# Modern
# Sports Science

LARRY KETTELKAMP

# Modern
# Sports Science

WILLIAM MORROW AND COMPANY, INC.
New York, New York

Printed in the United States of America.

1 2 3 4 5 6 7 8 9 10

Library of Congress Cataloging-in-Publication Data

Kettelkamp, Larry.
   Modern sports science

   Includes index.
   Summary: Describes how the body functions in athletic performance and dicusses the advances made in understanding muscle mechanics, body metabolism, peak performance, stress, mind and body relationships, and what is needed to become proficient in a sport.
   1. Sports sciences—Juvenile literature.   [1. Sports sciences. 2. Body, Human]  I. Title.
GV558.K47   1986      613.7′1     86-8754
ISBN 0-688-05494-3

J
613.7
KET

# Contents

# Acknowledgments

The author wishes to extend grateful thanks to the following specialists affiliated with The Institute for Medicine in Sports, Hamilton Square, NJ, for demonstrating equipment and techniques and offering critical and helpful suggestions:

Frank Barham, M.D.
G. Patrick Connors, A.T.C., M.Ed.
Richard Friscia, M.S., P.T., A.T.C.
Paul Maffei, D.P.M.
Eric Pallop, M.S., P.T., A.T.C.
Aaron Sporn, M.D.

Appreciation also is extended to the following persons and sources for providing information and contributing materials:

Melvin Ramey, Head Track Coach, University of California at Davis

Phil Swimley, Head Baseball Coach, University of California at Davis

Larry Ellis, Head Track Coach, Princeton University

Tom O'Connell, Head Baseball Coach, Princeton University

Richard F. Malacrea, M.S., R.P.T., Head Trainer, Princeton University

C. N. Stover, M.D., Hunterdon Orthopedic Associates, Flemington, NJ

Stephen Hefler, M.D., Princeton Junction, NJ

Lester Fehmi, Ph.D., Princeton Behavioral Medicine and Biofeedback Research Institute

Joseph D. Baylis, Star Fitness Center, East Windsor, NJ

To Jeff, Laurie, and Justin—
the "fitness family"

# Modern
# Sports Science

# Introduction

The human body is a capable and flexible organism. It adapts to a wide range of physical functions—from walking to running, jumping, climbing, and tumbling. It can propel itself smoothly through water and can perform intricate maneuvers in midair. It can handle tools and throw objects with exquisite precision. And it can exert forces or absorb impacts many times its own weight.

These capabilities and more are called into play by the varied demands of modern sports from baseball to hockey, from tennis to Olympic diving. There is satisfaction in encouraging the body to meet new goals and to surpass its own skills or compete with the skills of others in organized ways.

Understanding how the body functions in athletic

performance is a complex task and involves many professions. There is the role of the individual or team coach, the athletic trainer, the exercise specialist, the medical specialist, and those in the sciences who explore physiology and mechanics. Rapid and exciting advances have been made in understanding muscle mechanics, body metabolism, peak performance, stress, mind and body relationships, and the specifics needed to develop in a sports specialty. Sophisticated computer analysis has combined with refined training equipment and techniques. These advances have stimulated a surge of support for both amateur and professional athletics in the United States and around the world, resulting in a new discipline that can be called modern sports science. The chapters ahead discuss the parts of this new science and how they work together effectively.

*Note:* It is important to remember that all sports activities involve some risk. Any athletic training techniques, including those described in Chapter 3, should be undertaken only with a doctor's approval and with adequate coaching or supervision.

# 1/Body, Muscles, Bones, and Levers

The human body is a machine constructed of muscles, ligaments, tendons, and bones. Because of its complexity, it is helpful to break down the workings of this living machine into basics.

## PLANES AND JOINTS

Think of the body's structure in terms of three imaginary planes that pass through it and intersect each other. First, assume that the body is upright. One plane then runs from front to back and splits the body into its mirror halves. This is the *median plane.* The second imaginary plane is the *lateral plane.* It passes through the body from side to side, crossing the median plane at a right angle. The third, called the *horizontal plane,* passes across the midsection of the body parallel to the

3

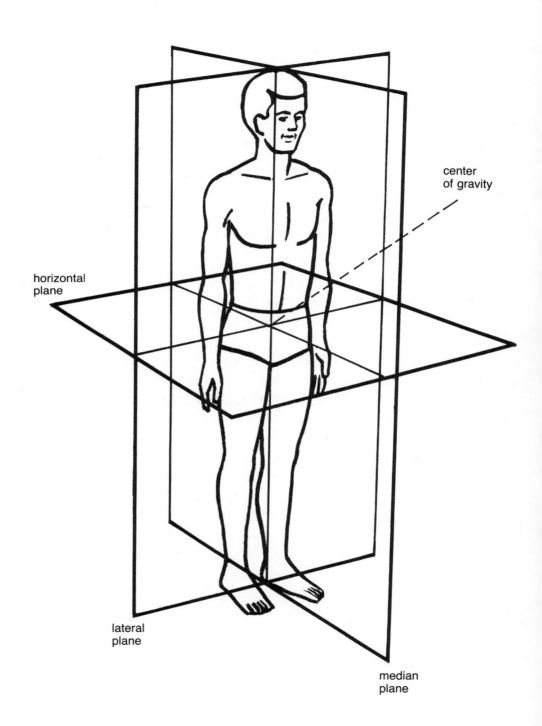

center
of gravity

horizontal
plane

lateral
plane

median
plane

floor and intersects both the median and lateral planes at right angles.

The three planes provide a basis for describing body motions. For example, in doing jumping jacks, arms and legs move out from the body and back along the lateral plane. In doing a jackknife from the diving board, the arms move down from overhead to touch the toes, and the body folds along the median plane. Or suppose arms are held out level from the shoulders and swung parallel to the floor. This is motion along the horizontal plane.

Several other terms help to describe body motions. Movement of an arm or leg away from the *midline*, or trunk of the body (as with the jumping jacks), is called *abduction*. And the movement back to the midline or trunk is called *adduction*. Some movements occur around a single point. For example, swinging your arm in a complete circle from the shoulder is called *circumlocution*. Other movements involve forms of rotation. You can rotate your wrist about your forearm to turn a doorknob. Or you can rotate your entire body around its vertical axis, the line where the median and lateral planes intersect. Folding motion, in which one body unit is bent against another, is called *flexion*. The opposite motion is *extension*, in which the flexed unit is

*Median, lateral, and horizontal body planes intersect at right angles at the center of gravity, the point at which all body parts balance exactly.*

returned to its unfolded position or beyond it. For instance, the swimmer who has flexed his body for the jackknife then extends it before entering the water. All of the complicated swinging, bending, twisting, kicking, jumping, and throwing motions of the body can be described as combinations of these basic motions.

*Jumping jacks use arm and leg abduction and adduction along the lateral plane.*

midline

Such actions are possible only because the body is constructed with many movable joints, which move in a variety of ways from simple to complex. The simplest possible joint movement is a gliding motion from side to side while bones stay at the same relative angles. Next is a simple bending motion in a single plane. Such a joint can work either like a hinge or like a rotating peg. Some joints permit action in two planes. These joints usually are shaped like an oval or a saddle. And finally, some joints permit movement in many direc-

*A jackknife uses a flexing motion along the median plane.*

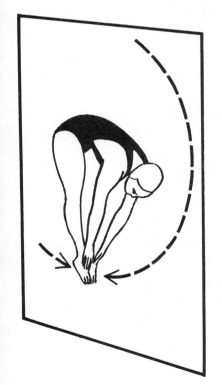

*Arm swings use movement along the horizontal plane.*

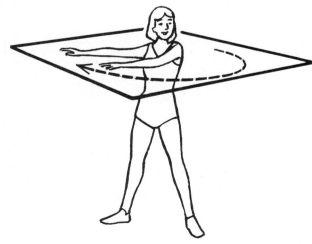

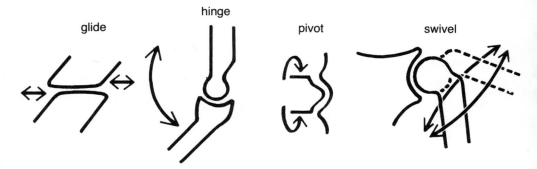

*Body joints permit many types of mechanical motion, from simple to complex.*

tions. They usually consist of a ball and socket that can swivel freely.

Body joints have stiff "articulating" cartilage between the bones, and flexible "fibrous" cartilage connecting the bones. The joints are wrapped by *synovial membranes,* or joint capsules, that contain *synovial fluid.* This lubricates the joints in much the same way that bearings hold oil around moving metal machine parts, thus protecting them from friction.

## LEVERS AND FORCES

The muscles and bones of the body work together as *levers.* A lever is a rigid bar that turns about a *pivot,* or *fulcrum,* when force is applied. The weight, or physical mass, that is set into motion is called the *resistance.* In the body each bone is a rigid bar, the movable joint connecting one bone to another is the fulcrum, and the muscles attached between them supply the force by contracting to change the angle of the rigid bars. The resistance may be the part of the body set into motion, a weight being held, or any other form of physical resistance. A simple example of this combination in action is the elbow joint of the arm. Two parallel bones in the forearm, the *ulna* and the *radius,* act as the bar of the lever. Ligaments at the elbow hinge these bones to the upper arm bone, called the *humerus.* The movable joint is the fulcrum. When the upper arm muscle, or *biceps,* contracts, it supplies a force on the forearm bones to pull them upward and flex the joint at the fulcrum, which is the elbow.

Another lever action takes place when the arm is straightened out. Suppose your arm is held overhead

*Simplified diagram of knee joint, showing bones, cartilages, ligaments, and tendons.*

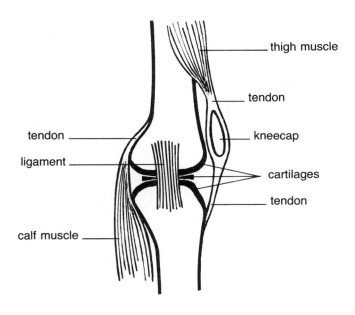

with elbow bent and pointing toward the ceiling. Your forearm bones now form the bar of a lever that can be moved in the opposite direction. This time the force is supplied by the contraction of the *triceps* muscle on the back of your upper arm. When the triceps contracts, the pulling force pivots the ulna away from the upper arm, raising your hand toward the ceiling to extend your arm.

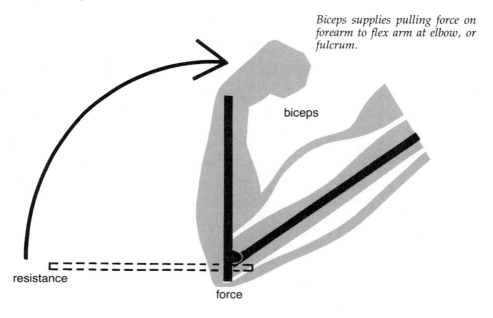

*Biceps supplies pulling force on forearm to flex arm at elbow, or fulcrum.*

biceps

resistance

force

fulcrum

The lever principle applies to all of the movable bones in your body. Sometimes there is a series of levers linked together. They can act both separately or together. The arm, for example, actually has a series of six levers.

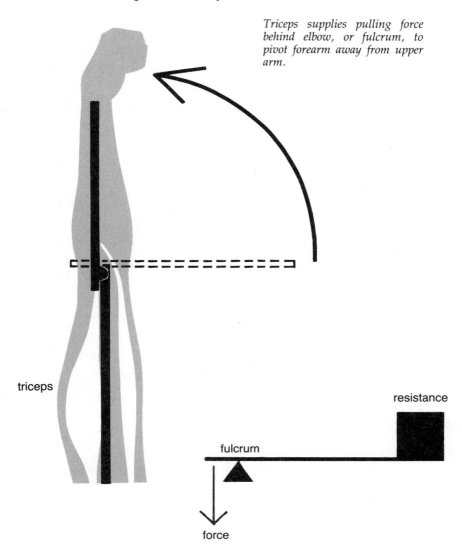

*Triceps supplies pulling force behind elbow, or fulcrum, to pivot forearm away from upper arm.*

triceps

resistance

fulcrum

force

First comes the upper arm, which is hinged to the trunk at the shoulder. Next comes the forearm, which was just described in the example. Hinged to this is the wrist, and connected in a series to it are the three small bones in each of the fingers.

The body machine can change the length of its levers by using tools and implements. A baseball bat is a lever. So is a golf club or a tennis racket. Suppose that you grip the handle of a tennis racket in one hand. In an overhand serve your upper arm and forearm act partly together. This can be considered as a lever that pivots from the shoulder. Your hand and the racket act partly together to form a second lever, hinged at the wrist. The racket that extends from your hand adds weight. Swinging the racket through the air adds wind resistance, and when the racket strings strike the tennis ball, resistance increases further. (Actually, in a tennis serve there is motion at all of the joints connecting arm, hand, and racket, but each section still acts as a mechanical lever.)

All body activities follow basic laws of motion. First, an object remains at rest until it is acted upon by a force. Second, the speed, or velocity, of a moving object depends on its weight, or mass, and the amount of force applied to it. Third, for every action there is an equal and opposite reaction.

Thus, more force must be applied to a heavy bowling ball than to a baseball to set it moving at the same speed. And anything you push against reacts in an equal and opposite way. For example, if a canoe paddle is pushed through the water, the canoe moves in one direction. At the same time the paddle displaces the water in the opposite direction. When you strike a baseball with sufficient force, the ball reacts by being moved away from the bat. But the bat is also pushed slightly back in relation to the ball, and this reactive force is transferred through the bat to your arms, shoulders, and trunk.

When you jump up from the earth, you actually push the earth away from you at the same time, but the earth is of such enormous size and mass that the effect cannot be measured. Nevertheless, because of its great mass, the earth also attracts you to itself, bringing still another force into play, the force of gravity, or *G-force*. In all sports activities gravity must be overcome in various ways. Suppose you do a high jump. First, a force must be exerted against the earth strong enough to set your body into forward motion, and at the point of the takeoff a greater force is applied to move your body away from the earth. However, gravity constantly supplies a force in the opposite direction. When it predominates, you land, and the force of the impact must be absorbed by your body. A similar action takes place when a track athlete throws the discus or tosses the shot put. The object is given momentum away from the earth, and the force of gravity pulls it back again.

Two additional components of motion are centrifugal force and centripetal force. These opposing forces centrifugal force          centripetal force

arise when an object is set into rotation. *Centrifugal force* is the tendency for the object to move out from a center. *Centripetal force* is the tendency for the object to move toward a center. When these forces balance, the object remains in rotation. A track athlete rotating, with a discus held at arm's length, develops both centripetal and centrifugal force. When centripetal force is removed as the discus is released, it then tends to fly off in a straight line. In the same way, a rotating line of skaters "cracking the whip" develops centrifugal force that gives high velocity to the skater who lets go of the line. A solo skater who does a spin is also using centrifugal force. The spin begins as a pivot with the free leg and both arms extended outward. The twist, or *torque*, from the pushoff gives a slow rotational speed to these body parts. Then, when the free leg is pulled in and the arms are pulled up over the head, centrifugal force is converted into increased rotational speed, or *angular momentum*.

When the human body is airborne, as in tumbling or diving, the same forces and laws of motion apply. In a forward flip with a half twist, for example, the aerialist first applies a force to the tumbling floor, div-

*Collegiate discus thrower. Centrifugal force counters centripetal force to keep the discus moving in a circular arc. When the discus is released, it tends to fly off in a straight line and curve into a ballistic path under the pull of gravity.*

ing board, or platform. The upward impetus is converted into a forward tuck and rotary motion about a horizontal axis. At the same time one arm is brought in across the chest, applying torque to start body rotation around a vertical axis. The result is a gracefully executed half twist, the coordinated combination of mechanical forces and laws of motion.

## MUSCLES AT WORK

Skeletal muscles are made of fibers that have the ability to contract or shorten when stimulated by nerve impulses. These impulses are programmed by the brain and routed through the spinal cord and peripheral nerves to muscles of head, neck, trunk, arms, and legs. When stimulated, a few or many muscle cells "fire" together or in sequence and the complex body machine is set into motion.

A muscle fiber at rest is loose and flexible. It can be stretched or pulled like a rubber band until it is per-

*Muscle fiber is able to contract to about half its resting length or stretch to half again its resting length.*

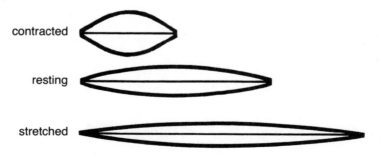

haps half again as long as it was at rest. Or, when stimulated to contract, it can bunch up to only about half the length of the resting state. This flexibility varies from person to person and can increase with training.

Skeletal muscles contain thousands of fibers grouped and overlapped according to the locations of muscles in the body and the jobs they have to do. The most basic muscle shape is like a teardrop or spindle, in which the muscle fibers all run generally in the same direction, as in the biceps of the upper arm. Other muscles have fibers grouped like the parallel ridges of a feather, radiating to one or both sides of a central line, as in certain muscles of the front of the thigh. Still others have fibers in a fan shape, as with the chest muscles, which radiate away from the shoulders and across the

*Muscle fibers are organized into basic shapes according to their functions and positions in the body.*

spindle
(as in biceps
of the arm)

featherlike
(as in quadriceps
of the thigh)

rectangular
(as in rhomboids
of the back)

fan-shaped
(as in pectorals
of the chest)

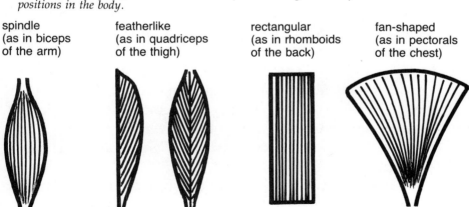

rib cage. And a few muscles are shaped much like a rectangle. Whatever their shapes and types, all muscles must be firmly anchored in order to do useful work. The bunched, contractile fibers of a muscle thin out toward each end to reveal a smooth core called *tendon*. The tendons in turn extend to anchoring points on the bones. Thus muscles and bones are permanently interlocked, ready to do the mechanical work of the body.

Muscle fibers have been found to be of many types. These are arbitrarily categorized as *slow-twitch* and *fast-twitch fibers*. Slow-twitch fibers are adapted for endurance. They contract slowly and are active in sustained activities such as swimming, running a long race, or lifting a heavy weight gradually. Fast-twitch fibers are adapted for rapid movements and a quick release of energy. They are used for bursts of activity such as a quick sprint or lifting a weight as rapidly as possible.

Every person is born with a certain proportion of slow-twitch to fast-twitch muscle fibers distributed throughout the body, and this ratio remains constant all through life. The person who happens to have more slow-twitch fibers than average may tend to be better at endurance sports, while the person who naturally has more fast-twitch fibers than average may tend to be better at short-term activities such as jumping, sprinting, or golfing.

Most slow-twitch muscle fibers are red, and most fast-twitch fibers are white. Apparently there are also red fast-twitch fibers as well as white fast-twitch fibers, and at least one type of fiber is of an intermediate slow-twitch type. Recent research shows that heavily used muscle fibers can actually split along their length, thus becoming more numerous. Nevertheless, the principle of a fixed ratio of slow-twitch fibers to fast-twitch fibers for each person still holds in a general way, and muscular training is based on this idea.

The contractile elements of muscle fibers, called *mibrofils*, can be altered through exercise. It is known that exercising with heavy weights or resistance at slow or moderate speeds will stimulate the slow-twitch fibers to become bulkier and stronger. On the other hand, the fast-twitch fibers also can be increased in bulk as well as strength by doing high-resistance exercises at fast speeds. This develops a power potential that is advantageous for almost any kind of athletic activity.

Skeletal muscles range in size from a fraction of an inch to one or two feet in length. All of these muscles have Greek or Latin names that are difficult to learn. However, an easy way to get some idea of the body's main muscle groups is to use their common abbreviations. Anyone who has been around a weight-training or bodybuilding gym has heard some of these terms.

*Pecs and Abs*

Pecs is short for *pectorals,* the large muscles that fan out from upper arms and shoulders to anchor on the breastbone, or *sternum*. They contract to pull, or adduct, the upper arms both downward toward the trunk and inward toward the chest. The pecs are at work in pushing and squeezing movements, such as doing push-ups or locking in an opposing linesman in football. Below the pecs are the abs, short for *abdominals*. These are the bumpy, double bands of muscle that connect the rib cage to the pelvic bones. They are at work in movements such as sit-ups or leg lifts, in which the trunk flexes forward toward the hips. Just beside the abs, on either side of the trunk, are the *oblique muscles*. These also connect rib cage to pelvis, but their contraction is involved in side bends or a twisting motion of the trunk to one side or the other. Together the pecs, abs, and obliques give the basic look to the trunk as seen from the front. On girls the pecs are partly covered by the breasts, but the muscles still do the same work.

### Traps, Lats, and Delts

Traps stands for *trapezius,* a large symmetrical set of muscles that connects the shoulder blades to the spine at the base of the skull and extends in two inverted trapezoids across and down the back to the spine. The upper division of the traps forms the triangular slope running from shoulders to neck. When this part contracts, the shoulders hunch up. When the lower parts contract, the shoulders and shoulder blades are pulled back and together and you "throw out" your chest.

Lats stands for *latissimus dorsi*. These are the muscles that give the tapered contour to the trunk as seen from the back. They, too, have a broad triangular shape and fan out from the upper arm to connect to the mid and lower parts of the spine. Their major action is to adduct the upper arms down and toward the trunk, as in bracing yourself upward on the arms of a chair or doing dips between parallel bars. Highly developed lats give a bodybuilder the wide "Superman" look.

Delts is short for *deltoids*. These are the muscles that cap the shoulders, connecting the upper arm to the upper ridge of the scapula and collarbone. The deltoids each have three sections, or *lobes*, and coordinate to lift, or abduct, the upper arms from front, side, and back. These muscles form the rounded shape of the shoulders, seen from both front and back.

### Biceps and Triceps

There are no common abbreviations for biceps and triceps. *Biceps* means "two heads," and it is the familiar two-part muscle that connects the lower arm to the top of the upper arm and shoulder blade. This is what you contract to "make a muscle" as you flex the forearm toward the upper arm. *Triceps* means "three heads," and it is the opposing three-part muscle on the back of the upper arm that straightens the elbow out again when it contracts. The triceps is horseshoe-shaped and

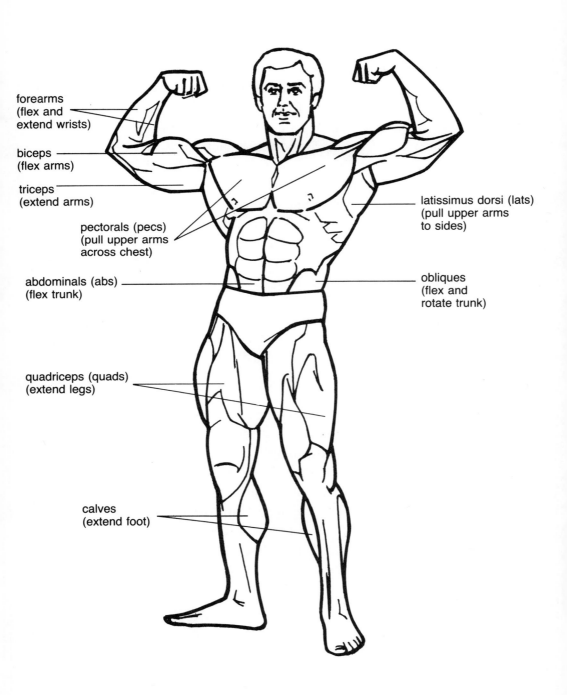

forearms
(flex and
extend wrists)

biceps
(flex arms)

triceps
(extend arms)

pectorals (pecs)
(pull upper arms
across chest)

abdominals (abs)
(flex trunk)

quadriceps (quads)
(extend legs)

calves
(extend foot)

latissimus dorsi (lats)
(pull upper arms
to sides)

obliques
(flex and
rotate trunk)

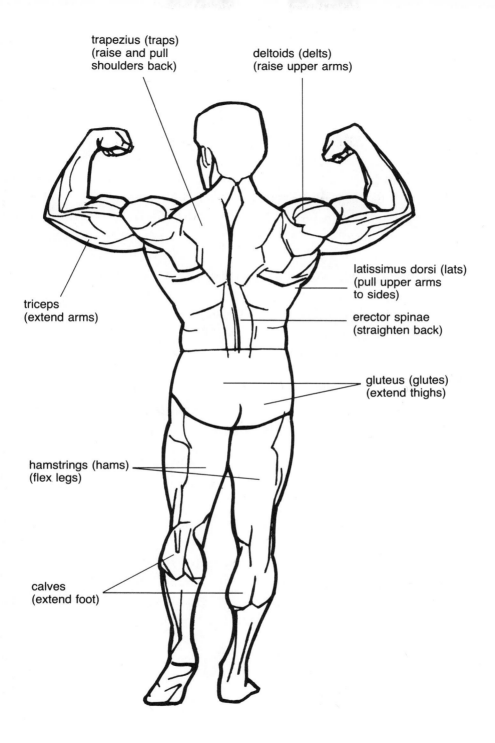

trapezius (traps)
(raise and pull
shoulders back)

deltoids (delts)
(raise upper arms)

latissimus dorsi (lats)
(pull upper arms
to sides)

triceps
(extend arms)

erector spinae
(straighten back)

gluteus (glutes)
(extend thighs)

hamstrings (hams)
(flex legs)

calves
(extend foot)

pops out visibly at the back of the arm when you do push-ups or shove yourself away from a desk.

### Quads and Hamstrings

Quads stands for *quadriceps,* a four-part muscle that gives the major shape to the front of the thigh. The quads straightens the knee, just as the triceps straightens the elbow. The *hamstrings,* or hams, are a group of three muscles on the back of the thigh, nicknamed because of their stringy tendons, which stretch across the back of the knee. The hamstring muscles contract to flex the knee. When you ride a bicycle, quads and hamstrings cooperate first to extend each knee, and then to flex it as you rotate the pedal sprocket.

### Glutes and the Erector Spinae

Glutes is short for *gluteus,* a group of three muscles that connects the pelvic bones to the upper thigh. These muscles rotate the pelvis in several ways, abduct the thigh, or extend the thigh toward the back, as a ballet dancer or figure skater does when standing on one leg and extending the other backward. The gluteus muscles give the major form to the hips as seen from the back and sides.

Above the gluteus muscles are the *erector spinae,* important muscles of the lower back that run vertically from the pelvis to the spine. As their name suggests, they contract to pull the spine erect and to maintain vertical posture. The erector spinae work in opposition to the abdominal muscles at the front of the lower trunk.

*Other Muscles*

Just as with the opposing muscles of upper arm or thigh, so there are also opposing groups of muscles at the front and back of the forearm and in the shin and calf of the lower leg. Those of the forearm move the wrist up or down. Those at the shin curl the foot upward, while those of the calf extend the foot as you do when raising up on your toes. In addition, many smaller muscles interconnect the tiny sectional joints of fingers and thumbs and the inner bones and toes of the feet. Above the trunk are special muscles to connect the skull to the collarbones and shoulder blades. These muscles move the head toward the trunk in any direction.

There are many more muscles that have not been named but which help lace together parts of the trunk and pelvis or assist muscles in the legs and arms that have already been described.

*Muscle Coordination*

Coordination of all the skeletal muscles is practiced from birth and improves with both maturity and training. Muscles contract in balanced relationships in response to intentions arising in the *cerebral cortex,* the highest center of your brain. On each side of the cortex are sections called the *motor strips,* where brain cells are organized to correspond to muscle groups of the body. The right half of the brain activates the left side of the body, and vice versa. There is constant feedback from nerves within the muscles and joints. This combines with information from the bodily senses of sight, sound, pressure, gravity, and balance. Thus the brain initiates body movement and continues to monitor, process, and control it.

## GROWTH AND STRENGTH

There always has been controversy about whether children and preteens should participate in certain sports activities. For example, is a Little League player likely to injure an arm that is not ready for pitching curves or sliders? Is a junior high football or soccer player more susceptible to injury than an eighteen-year-old? Can a sixth-grade girl safely enter a wrestling competition? Will a twelve-year-old boy injure bones or muscles by doing weight lifting?

The answers depend on many factors. First is an understanding of the physical changes that occur in a growing body. Not all parts develop or mature at the same rate. The bones of a newborn baby are soft and have gaps between them that will close as the bones grow and *ossify*, or harden. For example, the separate bones of the skull grow larger and harder until they finally touch, closing off the vulnerable soft spots that were between them in infancy.

The same hardening process gradually occurs in bones in the arms and legs. By the time a baby takes its first steps, the bones of the foot, lower leg, and thigh usually are strong enough to support the baby's weight. But at the knee joint certain small parts have not yet hardened or joined firmly to the larger bones around them. And the ligaments in the foot are still too flexible to hold the bones of the foot firmly in the proper relationships. Consequently, infants tend to be flat-footed. As ligaments become firmer and muscles get stronger, though, the foot develops a proper arch that can support body weight correctly.

By the time a youngster is six or seven years old, feet and ankles have developed enough to undertake all the normal demands of walking, running, and jumping. However, parts of the knee and elbow joints continue hardening and maturing all through the teen years and well into the twenties. For this reason almost all high school and even college athletes are still not completely physically mature.

Just as bones and joints continue to mature, the skeletal muscles and the nerves that activate them develop gradually at their own rate. A child's first movements are gross and clumsy. Over many years these become refined to highly skilled functions. The process never stops.

A crucial part of maturing comes with puberty. This is the time, usually between the ages of eleven and fourteen, when girls become women and boys become men. More of certain sex hormones and growth hormones are produced by the body. Breasts and genitals enlarge, and pubic hair appears. In girls the bones of the pelvis grow wider, and body fat is distributed differently. In boys the shoulders become wider, and muscles become larger.

Special chemicals called *androgens,* which are produced by the adrenal glands, trigger some of these changes. Androgens enable muscles to grow larger when they are stressed. Strenuously working a muscle actually causes some alteration of muscle tissue. However, with a sufficient supply of androgens the body is stimulated to synthesize protein so that not only is the tissue replaced, but also it becomes more massive.

Because this increase in androgen levels comes only with puberty, it has sometimes been assumed that training for muscle growth would not be effective in young children, and that special training for increased strength would not be worthwhile.

To test these assumptions a research program was set up in the Health and Physical Education Department at the University of Virginia in the summer of 1985. There Dr. Arthur Weltman organized volunteers into two test groups. The volunteers were boys between the ages of six and eleven who had not yet reached puberty. Nineteen of the boys were placed in a special training program. Another group of ten boys became what is called a *control group.* They received no training.

The training group underwent a fourteen-week program in which the boys met for three forty-five-minute sessions each week. Each session consisted of five to seven minutes of warm-ups and stretches, then thirty minutes of strength training, and finally five to seven minutes of cool-down exercises and more stretches.

The main part of each session was a workout on a series of exercise machines in which resistance to both pulling and pushing was provided by hydraulic cylinders. Eight stations were set up with one machine for each station, in order to exercise upper arms, forearms, chest, legs, hips, and shoulders in specific ways. Whenever possible, pulling and pushing motions were combined in a single exercise. Two extra exercises were added to the strength routine—sit-ups and stationary cycling—making a total of ten stations in all.

To complete a routine each boy exercised thirty seconds at one station, rested for thirty seconds, and then immediately moved to the next station. On the hydraulic machines each boy would do as many repetitions as possible in the thirty seconds. Whenever a boy was able to do thirty or more repetitions at a particular setting, the resistance would be increased to the next level on that machine. Each boy completed three circuits in a single session. During the fourteen-week test period the boys in training and those in the control group also participated in their usual organized sports.

Before and after the fourteen weeks of training, all the boys were tested in a number of ways. Strength was measured in arms, legs, shoulders, and trunk on a machine with a *dynamometer*, a device for computing mechanical force. Jumping ability was measured by having each boy do the standing long jump and the vertical jump. Flexibility was measured with a sit-and-reach test. In addition, body parts and sections were measured in circumference to see if size had increased or decreased. The density of fat-to-muscle was computed, the heart rate was monitored with an EKG machine, and *metabolism*, or the rate of the body's energy-burning systems, was tested with oxygen-consumption measurements and blood analysis. Bone scans were obtained to check for any hairline fractures caused by the training.

During the program the boys in the experimental group gained in all eight strength categories compared with those in the control group, who showed smaller gains, no gains, or even some losses in strength. The muscles in the trained youngsters did not get bigger, but they did become stronger. Further, the trained boys improved their oxygen consumption and their flexibility in lower back and legs. The parents of the trained boys reported that the boys performed better in their various sports as a result of the fourteen-week program. Bone and muscle tests showed only evidence of injuries that the boys were known to have received in their sports activities and not from the training.

The results of the study suggest that even concentrated strength training for children, combined with warm-ups and stretches, can be both safe and beneficial when it is carefully supervised.

Another question in athletics is whether women and girls should participate to the same extent as men and boys. The difference in the body build of young boys and girls is not marked. Most changes come with onset of puberty. Then, on the average, boys' shoulder structures broaden. With girls the shoulders change less, while hip structures widen to prepare for the possibility of eventual pregnancy. Girls tend to be taller than boys at the onset of puberty, but mature boys are taller, on the average, than mature girls. Girls generally have relatively longer trunks and shorter legs than boys, and with girls the inward angle of the legs from hip to knee is much greater because the thigh bones attach to a wider pelvis. These structural variations make for some natural differences in running and jumping abilities between males and females, with males taking advantage of their greater relative leg length. In addition, teenage girls are typically more loosely jointed than boys at ankles and shoulders, giving them the flexibility required for gymnastics. However, more knee injuries occur among female athletes than among male athletes.

Another very important difference between males and females is the amount and distribution of body fat. Females carry a greater proportion of fat to muscle, and the fat is deposited mainly between muscle and skin, giving women more natural buoyancy in water sports. Males have more muscle in proportion to fat, and the fat tends to be distributed within the muscles, giving men a power advantage in sports such as football and wrestling.

Of course, there are many exceptions to these averages. Women basketball players or volleyball players are tall, with legs longer than those of the average woman. Female runners may have very little body fat, and some women have exceptionally broad shoulders and narrow hips.

Since women develop breasts, it has often been assumed that they are more susceptible to upper body injury in contact sports. However, doctors who treat women athletes report no unusual injuries to women's breasts as a rule. Complaints usually come from friction and skin irritation due to poorly fitting bras.

When young women take up serious sports, it may affect the onset of *menses,* or the monthly period. The beginning can be delayed to as late as age sixteen to eighteen. Or if a young woman has begun menses and then takes up sports, menses may become irregular or even stop when training is stressful. Sometimes these changes can also come from poor diet or emotional factors. If a young woman is healthy, there is no apparent

*Flo Hyman, at right, uses her height and jump advantage to spike the ball as the U.S. Women's Volleyball Team competes against Cuba in the 1984 Olympic Games.*

harm from delayed menses, and starting menses late does not reduce chances of becoming pregnant later.

The average difference in muscle-to-fat ratio between men and women means that most men are stronger and faster than women of similar height and body weight. For this reason there are separate women's sports teams, and separate women's and men's events in sports such as track and tennis. And in ballet and couples skating it is the man who lifts the woman and not the other way around. In general men and women are not built alike, and it makes sense to respect these differences when organizing competitive sports. However, there has been pressure for many sports to go coed, and there is no reason for this not to happen as long as skills are more or less equal. Certainly any athlete, whether male or female, is only going to have a full opportunity if training is extended equally to both sexes.

Movies and television have popularized the idea that a girl can be as good as a boy at pitching in the Little League. Recently a girl went out for the boys' football team at a high school in New Jersey. Her ability and strength were not as fully developed as those of the boys. Nevertheless, she remains on the team, since school policy dictates that no one who goes out for football will be cut from the full squad. As the only girl on the team, she does the same calisthenics, time sprints, blocking, tackling, and catching exercises as the rest of her teammates.

In another coeducational sports venture begun in the fall of 1985, five senior boys were allowed to join the girls' field hockey team at a high school in Massachusetts. The boys had excellent speed, but as novice hockey players, they needed to acquire the skills the girls had developed through their years of training and experience.

An example of concentrated training that can be undertaken by young people is the Gymnastics Academy in Eugene, Oregon, run by Dick Muldihill, coach of many Olympic gymnasts. Girls and boys of ages twelve or thirteen enroll in the program. Some students whose families live at a distance actually stay in dorms at the facility. All students undergo six hours of supervised training and four hours of school every day. Despite the intense schedule, the gymnasts develop skills and strength slowly and methodically, receiving careful attention to both technique and safety. The success of the program is shown by the number of students who remain in training and go on to careers in competitive gymnastics.

Nevertheless, sometimes the demands of athletic competition can be too severe for the developing bodies of young athletes. An example is rotational injury to the knee or elbow, where bone closure is still incomplete. Such injuries may occasionally occur in the throwing arms of Little League baseball players or in the elbows of young gymnasts. For instance, one recently developed maneuver in competitive gymnastics

*At* left, *Yolande Mavity, 14, USA and World Championships team member.*
*At* right, *Ricardo Casis, 13, Junior National team member.*

*Both young gymnasts train at the National Academy of Artistic Gymnastics in*
*Eugene, Oregon, producer of such Olympic champions as Tracee Talevera and*
*Julianne McNamara.*

consists of a vault combining two forward somersaults
with a full twist, all executed in the air. The severe
rotation placed on the arms and elbows at the moment
of impact on the vaulting horse can cause joint injury.
In some instances surgery has permitted young athletes to recover from such injury and return to training
and competition.

Clinics devoted to specialized screening and testing
of junior-high and high-school-age athletes have begun to appear in major cities such as New York, Los
Angeles, and Cleveland. These include not only med-

ical examinations but also tests for skeletal and muscular strength as well as overall physical fitness. The results have been such general recommendations as leg stretches for all young athletes, or suggestions for specific sports such as limiting young baseball players to no more than 120 pitches per week.

Thus there is agreement that there are limitations to the performance expectations of young athletes in certain demanding situations. And these factors must be taken into account in planning programs of physical development for growing youngsters. However, most experiments suggest that there is no reason for any normal male or female, whether youngster or adult, not to participate in a chosen sport to the level of his or her capacity, providing there is no medical restriction and that adequate training and supervision are available.

# 2/Food for Sport

## NUTRITION

In a real sense you are what you eat, and everything you do depends on what you eat. Especially when called upon for sports activities, the body must be well and correctly fed. This involves principles of basic nutrition.

There are three essential food groups: carbohydrates, fats, and proteins. These are supplemented by the vitamins and minerals needed in small amounts to trigger efficient use of foodstuffs. And these cannot be useful without the intake of water, the main substance of the body. Water serves as a basis for all the fluid systems, such as blood and lymph, as well as for cellular chemical reactions involving growth, repair, the

38

elimination of wastes, and the conversion of raw material into energy.

Carbohydrates take the form of starches or sugars and are found in grains, milk, vegetables, and fruit. Fats are found in foods such as butter, cream, meats, nuts, and olives. Both carbohydrates and fats are energy foods for the body. Fats provide about twice as much fuel energy as the same amount of carbohydrates but require more steps to convert since they are held in storage.

Sugars taken into the body can be metabolized or burned quickly. They are good as quick-energy foods. Carbohydrates are digested into sugars such as glucose or can be stored by the body as glycogen in the liver and in muscle tissue. Fats are stored both under the skin as well as between muscle tissues and various organs of the body. The body not only stores fats taken in directly but synthesizes fats from any of the other types of food. For instance, sugar not used immediately for energy is converted to fat and stored.

The third major food group are the proteins. Proteins can be used as an energy source, but mainly they are the building materials of the body's tissues. Proteins are found in various animal parts and products such as lean meat, fowl, fish, dairy products, eggs, and also in legumes such as peas and beans.

For a balanced diet some foods from each of the three basic groups should be eaten each day.

There is disagreement over the exact amounts of vitamins and minerals required by the body. Modest amounts of the various vitamins are either manufactured by the body or taken in to assist in food metabolism. Vitamin A aids maintenance of skin and mucous membranes. The B-vitamin group is involved in the metabolism of protein, carbohydrates, and fats. Vitamin C has a role in oxygen-reduction metabolism and the maintenance of connective tissue. Vitamin D is essential for bone development. Vitamin E helps with the storage of vitamin A and aids skin maintenance, and vitamin K is involved with the clotting of blood. Other natural chemicals such as choline, folic acid, lecithin, and pantothenic acid have been found helpful in body metabolism, growth, or repair, and additional vitamin-like substances continue to be isolated. Some athletes have experimented with large doses of various vitamins, but there is no real evidence that more than modest daily amounts are needed, and sometimes extreme dosages can actually be harmful.

The body also requires small amounts of many minerals. Some, such as calcium, phosphorus, and molybdenum, are essential for the development of bones and teeth. Iron is essential for red blood cells so they can carry oxygen. Others, such as iodine, magnesium, manganese, and potassium, are active in body metabolism or muscle contraction. As many as fifty minerals are found as minor, or tracer, elements in body and brain, all playing some role in maintaining good health.

The mineral sodium, or salt, is needed in modest amounts to regulate fluid levels in the body and to stimulate nerve activity. Salt is easily lost through sweating, and athletes once were encouraged to take salt tablets in hot weather to avoid heatstroke. However, recent studies show that excess salt is linked with heart disease. Dr. Gabe Mirkin, a popular marathon runner, radio host, and sports physician, points out that long-distance runners on regular low-salt diets may actually have an advantage. This was pointed up in 1967 during the running of the National AAU thirty-kilometer marathon. The race happened to be held in extremely hot weather, and a mathematician named Tom Osler won the event in a surprising upset. Osler had been on a low-salt diet. Tests for sodium loss were made on a number of runners, and it was found that those who had been taking additional salt excreted large amounts of this mineral in sweat and urine, actually causing a salt deficit. Osler, on the other hand, excreted very little salt because it was being retained by the sweat glands, apparently giving him the advantage in the hot-weather marathon.

Many physicians insist that a well-balanced diet will provide all the basic vitamins and minerals that are necessary for anyone in any situation. Others believe that the stress of sports competition increases many vitamin and mineral requirements. Particularly, physicians with an emphasis in nutritional medicine believe that a balanced supplement of vitamins and minerals, preferably in natural form with their associated substances, should be part of the daily intake of athletes and nonathletes alike.

## ENERGY AND ENDURANCE

Almost all of the energy burned by the body eventually is converted to heat, and standard units of measure have been developed to monitor this process. The amount of heat required to raise one gram of water one degree Centrigrade is called a *calorie;* and the amount of heat required to raise the temperature of one kilogram of water one degree Centrigrade is 1000 gram calories. This unit is called a kilogram calorie, or kilocalorie. It is the common unit used to measure the heat energy released by various foods and is usually simply called a calorie for convenience.

An average adult male burns about 2000 calories per day just to remain awake and alive. Beyond this subsistence level, every physical activity makes additional calorie demands. For example, walking or riding a bike slowly burns about 210 extra calories per hour. Swimming burns around 300 calories per hour, while ice skating burns about 400 and playing tennis about 420. Skiing can burn around 600 calories, and running can use up to 900 or more calories per hour. Of course, the number of calories burned also varies with the intensity of each activity.

An athlete who is overweight needs to burn more calories than he or she takes in. However, if weight is lost only through dieting, some muscle tissue will be lost along with excess body fat, since the body does not discriminate among energy reserves. Proper exercise along with calorie regulation ensures that muscle tissue and strength are maintained while body weight drops. On the other hand, a football tackle may want to maintain body weight or actually increase it by boosting calorie intake along with regular exercise. Thus strength and muscle weight increase along with overall body weight.

Foods taken into the body are not burned directly for energy. Instead, the body cells depend on a chemical called *adenosine triphosphate,* or *ATP.* "Tri" means that there are three phosphate compounds in ATP. Whenever one of these breaks away, energy is released and ATP changes to *adenosine diphosphate,* or *ADP,* which has only two phosphate compounds. ADP in turn reacts with foodstuffs to release energy that converts the ADP back into more ATP. Still another chemical compound in the cells, *phosphocreatine,* or *PC,* is also involved in energy transfer and energy release. The various chemical exchanges within the cell combine to convert food to useful energy for muscle contractions, nerve impulses, and other functions.

There are three basic systems that supply fuel for body activity. The first is called the *ATP-PC system.* This is a rapid exchange in which PC is broken down so that its phosphorus can combine with ADP to make ATP. The rapid burst of energy released is used by muscles for activities that last only about ten seconds or less.

A second chemical exchange is called the *lactic acid system*. It starts with a sugar called *glucose*, the most common component of carbohydrates. Glucose is broken down into pyruvic acid, which unites mainly with hydrogen. In this process ATP is formed, and a product called lactic acid remains. The energy released by this fuel-burning system can be used for muscular activities lasting from one to three minutes.

Both the ATP-PC system and the lactic acid system supply fuel to the muscles for only very short times. For example, the ATP-PC system might supply most of the energy for a 100-yard dash, while the lactic acid system could provide energy to complete an 880-yard run. These systems do not involve oxygen, so they are called *anaerobic*, which means "without air." When athletic activities last longer than a few minutes, however, a third system is brought into play. This system is called *aerobic* because it involves the burning of oxygen, which is essential for long-term energy. A cross-country ski race, for example, would rely heavily on this system. In a typical aerobic event, heart rate is raised to about 160 beats per minute, and energy is expended continually in low amounts. Oxygen taken in by the lungs is carried through the bloodstream to muscle cells. There the oxygen is used to break pyruvic acid down into carbon dioxide and water, which are exhaled. The energy released is used to synthesize large amounts of

ATP, which then supplies the direct energy source for the muscles.

Most sports require some combination of anaerobic and aerobic energy systems. In football, short runs or blocks would be mostly anaerobic, while running a pass pattern or returning a punt would include some aerobic activity as well. A 500-yard swim would be about half aerobic and half anaerobic. An ice hockey player shifting constantly from one end of the ice to the other would be operating essentially aerobically, adding bursts of anaerobic energy during intense drives.

During the energy conversion process the body is using reserves of carbohydrates and fats in varying amounts, depending on the length of the athletic activity. For about the first hour of exercise the body burns mostly carbohydrates. If the activity continues past about an hour and fifteen minutes, the amount of available carbohydrates will have dropped rapidly. To continue moving the body increases the rate at which it burns fats. And in sessions that stretch out over more than two hours, as in a soccer practice, for example, the body begins depending on reserves of glycogen, or carbohydrate, stored in the liver as a source of energy. The liver is the organ that has been supplying glycogen for the bloodstream to carry to the muscles, and now its temporary storage supply is being depleted.

One benefit of endurance training is that the body gradually is trained to store and burn fuel more efficiently. If an athlete exercises muscles to exhaustion and then eats carbohydrate-rich foods, the muscles can be trained to hold up to three times the usual amount in the form of glycogen, the muscle's basic carbohydrate storage substance. Endurance training also triggers production of more enzymes, the proteins that stimulate chemical interactions, to help burn fat. The muscle of a trained athlete can burn fat at up to seven times the rate this occurs in an untrained muscle. Burning additional fat spares the glycogen reserves and allows the athlete to perform much longer before becoming exhausted. Such a change in the balance of carbohydrate-to-fat consumption occurs in the trained runner who is able to stretch energy reserves for a marathon.

Endurance also depends on the body's ability to deliver oxygen to the muscles. This is measured by the *oxygen volume maximum*, or $VO_2$ max. The $VO_2$ max is related to the strength of the heart muscle, the size and number of the blood channels, the number of red cells in the blood, and the rate at which enzymes in the muscles pick up oxygen from the blood.

The resting heart rate of an untrained person is about 75 beats per minute, and the maximum heart rate is about 190 beats per minute. In a fully trained athlete the resting heart rate is perhaps as low as 50, and the maximum heart rate can increase to 200 or more. At the same time the $VO_2$ max for an untrained male, measured in *METs*, or metabolic equivalents, the standard units of oxygen consumption, is around 38, while that of the trained athlete is around double that figure. For example, the $VO_2$ max of former long-distance runner and record holder, Steve Prefontaine, was measured at 84.3.

The reason for these dramatic changes in heart rate is that regular and vigorous athletic training causes the heart muscle to enlarge and to become stronger. The arteries leading away from the heart become larger than normal in order to handle an increased volume of blood, and the number of small blood capillaries increases. At the same time the total number of oxygen-carrying red blood cells also can increase along with the capacity of the metabolic system to use the available oxygen. The fuel-burning machinery of the body has thus doubled its efficiency. The stronger heart pumps fewer times per minute, and the whole cardiovascular system is healthier.

BODY CYCLES

Just as the body depletes certain energy resources more rapidly than others, it takes varying amounts of time to replenish these reserves. Suppose you have competed in a cross-country event. Depending on the distance and the amount of fatigue you experience, it will take anywhere from a day to several weeks to recover your normal energy levels. The glycogen depleted from the muscles and the liver will take from about ten hours to ten days to replenish. Potassium, the important mineral released in converting ATP to energy in the muscles, will take two full days to replace. Potassium replacement is especially important, since this mineral widens the blood vessels and helps to carry unwanted heat away from the muscles. Magnesium, essential to muscle contraction, is lost through sweat and other waste products, and also must be replaced. Furthermore, muscle tissue itself regularly becomes damaged even though there are no obvious injuries. The repair time depends on the kind of breakdown that has occurred and how much tissue is affected.

For these reasons your body needs to be paced with cycles of activity and rest. It is a good idea to alternate hard days with easy days. A hard day consists of activity that raises the average heart rate to between 120 and 180 beats per minute during an intense workout. The body is stressed by pushing muscles to the maximum for a short time. On an easy day the activity is much less intense. Low demands are placed on the muscles, and heart rate rises only slightly.

An example of pacing would be to train with weights or resistance machines every other day for three days out of the week. In between the heavy workout days activities could consist of walking, cycling, or other recreational sports. Or, as another example, pacing for a professional football team might begin with a game on Sunday. Then on Monday only light-drill and stretching exercises are planned. Tuesday is the players' day off. Wednesday is a hard game-practice day.

On Thursday and Friday only moderate or light practices are scheduled. Finally, Saturday is either a day for travel or a day off. The weekly schedule may also include in-season weight training, with routines tailored to individual needs.

The pacing cycles can have all kinds of variations. The important principle is to alternate activity and rest, as well as to alternate heavy stress with low stress. This way physical condition and skills are maintained while the body has a chance to repair and rebuild itself and to replace its energy resources.

Another type of planning is especially useful for widely spaced competition. This alternates background training with peak training. Background training can last for several weeks to many months. During this period the overall emphasis is on frequent periods of heavy work loads that stress the muscles and cardiovascular system to improve strength, muscle size, and the ability to metabolize fuels and oxygen. Then, from two to six weeks before the event, the training is changed to lighter workout loads, done more rapidly and repeated more times in the same period.

One of the most constant body energy cycles is that of the twenty-four-hour day. Every person has an individual temperature peak during waking hours, usually sometime between early and late afternoon. This coincides with the time when metabolism is most efficient and is the time when energy will be highest for that person and athletic performance optimum.

Various body systems also have their own twenty-four-hour pacing. Nutritionists Harvey and Marilyn Diamond report that the digestive system undergoes an elimination cycle from about 4 A.M. to noon, and an acquisition cycle from about noon to 8 P.M. They suggest that fruits are best eaten in the morning since they require less energy to be assimilated, and that proteins and carbohydrates are best eaten in the afternoon or evening when digestion is more active and can efficiently break down the more complex foodstuffs in a shorter period of time.

While protein from meats, dairy products, or vegetables is important to enable body tissues to build and repair themselves, only moderate regular amounts are needed by any athlete. Beyond this, extra protein is not used by the body. Some players still eat a steak before a big game. But recent research shows that eating carbohydrates—starchy foods such as potatoes and spaghetti—provides more of the nutrients needed for a sports competition.

In 1967 two Swedish scientists, Eric Hultman and Per-Olof Åstrand, developed a system of energy cycling called *carbohydrate packing,* or *loading.* Six days before an event an athlete trains so hard that his or her muscles are exhausted. This is called the *depletion phase.* For the next three days the athlete eats meals mainly of protein and fat, such as steak, chicken, fish, eggs, or cheese. Then, for the following three days, he packs with carbohydrates by eating many small meals that include high-calorie sugars and starches, such as bread and butter, cheese and tomatoes, chicken breasts, potatoes, noodles, peanut butter, and bananas.

A study done by Paul Slovic in 1975 showed that marathon runners shortened their race times by an average of eleven minutes by using Åstrand's six-day system. Many athletes and coaches now believe that the depletion phase is not needed, since depletion occurs regularly when athletes are in serious training. However, there is general agreement that a carbohydrate-packing cycle just before a big event is one of the best ways to guarantee optimum performance.

# 3/Sports Training

BIOMECHANICS

Athletic preparation for sports competition has undergone rapid changes. Today, advanced technology is applied to the measurement and evaluation of body motions and body functions to test fitness, athletic capability, and skill levels for specific sports. A new science has emerged called *biomechanics*. It employs high-speed film or videotape of athletes in motion and mathematical analysis of moving points on parts of the body. It involves computerized measurements of muscle contraction, pressure changes, and forces acting on and within the body. Biomechanics combines with exercise physiology to include the monitoring of breathing, heart rate, and the calculation of calories burned as fuel. In short, the new technology spans the coor-

52

*Human body model used to compute complex athletic motions.*

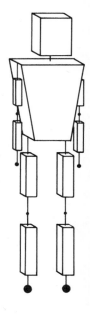

dinated study of the body as a machine of action and energy.

This improved scientific knowledge has been applied in a revolutionary way to training in every aspect of sports. An example of the usefulness of biomechanics comes from the University of California at Davis. Beginning in 1971, the head track coach, Melvin Ramey, and the baseball coach, Phil Swimley, both carried out independent studies. As well as being track coach, Ramey is a civil engineer. He used his engineering background to study motion pictures of his long jumpers. A mechanical body model was used to simulate the stages of the long jump. Ramey applied mathematical formulas to body movements and concluded that the most useful approach was to treat the

Above: *Simulated long jump using standard "hitch kick" during flight.*

Below: *Simulation of experimental somersault long jump not yet permitted in international competition. Long curves show ballistic trajectories. Dotted lines of stick figures show left arm and leg.*

long jump as a ballistic motion. He computed the path the jumper's body followed as it was propelled away from the earth and then returned to it, and related this to the mechanical forces applied to the jumper's body. Ramey found that some jumpers were not moving in the most efficient way for the ballistic trajectory. He was able to suggest changes in technique that were effective for his own athletes and also for other long jumpers who came to the campus for assistance.

At around the same time U.C. at Davis baseball coach Phil Swimley made a revolutionary discovery in examining the biomechanical motion of pitching an overhand curve ball. San Francisco Giants pitcher Ron Bryant, a right-hander, had come to the Davis campus between seasons to work on his curve ball delivery.

Above: *Imagined curve ball delivery assumes that wrist rotates* clockwise, *leaving hand palm-up after the ball has been thrown.*

Swimley had access to a high-speed camera capable of taking 3,000 frames per second and filmed Bryant's curve ball. The characteristic feeling in curve ball delivery is that the ball is released as the wrist rotates to the *right* and follows through to leave the hand palm-up. The camera showed that what really happened was that the moment the ball was released at the top of the swing, the hand first rotated to the *left*, palm-down, and continued to twist over entirely. At this point the elbow was bent up and out, and the hand position was exactly opposite that of the imagined delivery. Then, in order to follow through as taught, Bryant actually "derotated" his wrist a half circle in the other direction. The extra rotation took place only after the ball had been released.

imagined curve ball delivery

Below: *High-speed camera frames show that the elbow actually is raised and the wrist rotates* counterclockwise *after ball is released. Clockwise follow-through is unnecessary and can damage shoulder.*

actual curve ball delivery

*Collegiate baseball pitcher prepares to release a breaking pitch.*

Both Swimley and Bryant were amazed. To verify what they saw in the high-speed photographs, Swimley photographed the curve delivery of a series of pitchers selected from the major leagues, minor leagues, and college teams. The unusual reverse rotation was the same for the curve ball delivery in all the pitchers.

Swimley concluded that the extra, or opposite, rotation added to the end of the curve ball delivery was not only unnecessary but also could be harmful to the shoulder. The unneeded rotation twists the wrist 180 degrees in about 3/2000 of a second, and the shoulder rotates in the same direction. Three muscles of the shoulder join in a tendon that attaches to the humerus, or upper arm bone. In an overhand throwing motion the tendon rubs against an arching ligament that covers the shoulder joint. Unneeded friction can cause tears in this area. Although Swimley's surprising discovery has not been readily accepted, the scientific evidence demonstrates that changes in pitching technique can reduce the risk of serious shoulder injury, perhaps extending careers.

Technical breakthroughs have occurred in the analysis of foot and leg motion in recent years, as well. One example is a system designed by The Langer Biomechanics Group. It consists of a computer console and keyboard, a computer printer, a portable waist pack, and sensors placed on the feet. This system can be

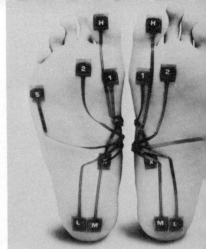

At left, *an enlarged Langer EDG force sensor.*
Right, *sensors placed at pressure points on bottoms of feet.*

used by anyone—from children to adults and from athletes to those with severe walking, posture, or foot problems.

Typically a sample reading is first taken in a physician's office. The portable computer pack, which weighs only six ounces, is strapped to the waist at front or back. Wires that look like coiled phone cords run from the waist pack to cushioned ankle straps. From there, thin individual wires connect to sensors placed on the bottom of each foot.

Each sensor is a thin, pressure-sensitive computer element about one-half-inch square. Up to seven microsensors are placed on the bare sole of each foot at special weight-bearing points. When a person walks barefoot for thirty seconds, the entire pattern of foot-to-ground action can be monitored and stored by the computer waist pack.

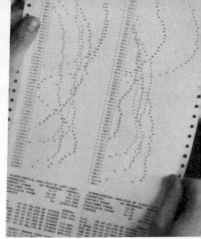

Left, *a computer stores patient's medical history and analyzes data collected from force sensors during "30-second walk."*

*At* right, *an EDG computer printout.*

Whenever a foot strikes the ground, the heel touches first. Two sensors there sample the pressure, recording the point at which the heel bears the greatest weight and when it passes the weight forward. Other sensors at the middle of the foot and then at the toes immediately register further pressure changes as the foot rolls both forward and from side to side in the complex pattern of walking.

After a sample walk is completed, the waist pack is removed and connected to the computer console. Data from the sensors stored over the thirty-second time period is transferred to the computer where general medical information about the patient already has been entered and stored. The combined information generates a printer readout, which includes an extended series of pressure readings from the sensors on each foot.

The Langer Company has named the computer print-out an Electrodynogram®, or EDG for short.

Normally the foot shares the weight load by distributing it along its length during the act of walking. The printout shows which pressure points are doing their share or which are bearing too much or too little weight. These details are revealed in a way that is not possible for the human eye to observe. Corrections can then be calculated that may necessitate inserting individually prescribed forms, called *orthotics*, in particular parts of the shoes.

An advantage of the system is that the waist pack is portable. Sensors can be worn inside a pair of shoes at work, athletic activities, or recreation. When the waist pack is returned to the physician's office, the data is plugged into the computer for a new readout.

The United States Olympic Committee in Colorado Springs has used the EDG system to make biomechanical measurements of Olympic race walkers. In this marathon sport contestants must walk rather than run. Walkers use a style in which arms pump vigorously, hips swivel from side to side, and one foot always touches the ground. With the computer printouts coaches have been able to evaluate race walking technique and to help walkers modify their styles in order to improve race times and reduce the risk of foot and leg fatigue and injury.

The EDG is one of a number of sophisticated devices now in use at U.S. Olympic facilities in Colorado

*Race walker wears Langer EDG waist pack. Computer stores electrical signals from pressure sensors placed on bottom of feet inside shoes.*

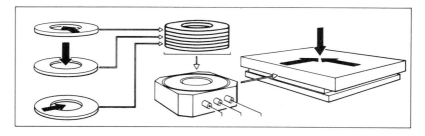

*Discs of quartz crystal, which generate electricity when stressed in a certain direction, are cut and stacked inside force platform at right. Unit measures forces that travel downward, side to side, and forward and backward.*

Springs. The USOC Department of Biomechanics and Computer Services was set up in 1981 to establish a center for advanced biomechanical research. Most of the equipment has been donated by manufacturers in return for test information that helps them to update their products. USOC services include five basic techniques. The first is high-speed filming and video imaging, both of which serve as a basis for detailed motion analysis. Next comes force platform studies, one of the most well-established methods of biomechanical measurement. A force platform is a stationary plate that responds to the dynamically shifting forces of foot contact. Individual layers of quartz within the plate generate an electric current when stressed horizontally or vertically. The plate can be imbedded in a floor or running track, for example, to measure the forces of a sprinter crossing it, or a shot-putter or archer standing on it while body weight shifts.

Closely coordinated with force plate measurements are the more detailed studies of foot pressure and gait made with the EDG equipment. The USOC lab also uses high-tech equipment to analyze moving points of light. Light-emitting diodes, or LEDs, are attached to parts of an athlete's body. As he or she moves, the

Above left: *Clear, red, and green light-reflecting prisms.*

Above right: *Prisms attached at ankle, knee, and hip (actually on opposite side of runner) reflect light beams to scanner on table.*

Below left: *Powerful lights are directed by three rotating mirrors to sweep field of view. Light reflected by colored prisms is returned along paths of mirror beams and coded to compare color and position.*

Below right: *Computer generates "stick-figure" action display of one leg pushing off.*

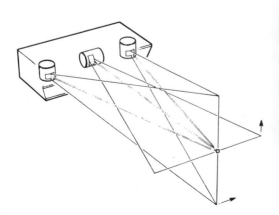 

paths of the moving red lights are picked up by one or more infrared-sensitive cameras and displayed on a computer screen. By locating LEDs at wrist, shoulder, hip, knee, and ankle, for example, the computer images can be used to construct animated stick figures of body movements, revealing errors in athletic technique. Other equipment is used to monitor muscle firing. With these, electrical sensors fastened to the body transmit signals to a recorder.

*Athletic activities analyzed from high-speed motion pictures. Major body points are connected and plotted by computer to form sequences of stick figures.*

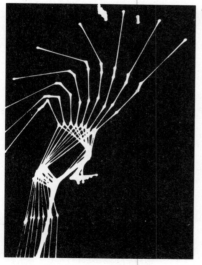

tennis serve

   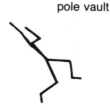 

pole vault

The sophisticated biomechanical techniques were offered to gifted athletes in the Elite Athlete Program, organized in 1981. The project coordinated research at Colorado Springs with that submitted by facilities in colleges and labs across the United States. By 1983, it encompassed fifteen separate programs, including twenty-two different sports, ranging from archery, bobsledding, and cycling, to ice hockey, rowing, and weight lifting.

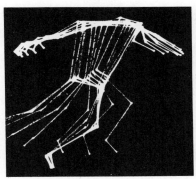
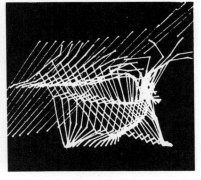

discus throw                    javelin toss

*Charles Dillman, head of the Department of Biomechanics, operates a computer console at U.S. Olympic Training Center in Colorado Springs, Colorado.*

One important part of biomechanical analysis is the measurement of G-forces. It is customary to think of these in terms of astronauts being launched into space, but the same principle applies to athletic movements. One G is the force of gravity pulling against you when you are standing motionless on the earth. Two Gs would be double that force, and so on. If you accelerate away from the earth, the G-forces increase, and if you fall back toward the earth, the G-forces decrease.

This is what happens to a pole vaulter, for example. His forward motion down the runway and his step-off transfer a force to the vaulting pole as a lever. This force, plus that contributed by the flexible pole, must be sufficient to accelerate his body weight upward against increasing G-forces. At the top of the arc he begins a free-fall back to the earth. And as he lands in the pit the air cushions must help his body to again absorb the extra G-forces of the impact.

Normally G-force is greatest in the part of the body receiving impact, and for a runner or jumper this force is applied to the feet and ankles. An exception is jumping on a trampoline, and this difference was first measured as part of government research into space flight and weightlessness.

G-force measurements were made at the Biomechanical Research Division of the NASA–Ames Research Center in California. The tests compared jumping vertically on a treadmill with jumping on a rebounder. G-force was measured with accelerometers attached to three points on the body: ankle, back, and forehead. On the solid surface, G-force measured at the ankle was more than twice that measured at the back and the forehead. However, on the trampoline, the G-force was almost equally distributed at all three points. Stress from jumping or rebounding can be as high as 8 Gs. The risk of cell rupture was much lower on the rebounder because of the equal distribution of G-forces. A conclusion of the tests was that astronauts exposed to weightlessness could safely use rebounders for deconditioning. Similar advantages apply to those who exercise either at home on a rebounder or in a gym on a

*Rebounder offers advantages of aerobic exercise with G-forces distributed almost equally throughout body.*

trampoline. Not only is stress distributed away from feet and ankles, but the alternation of G-forces throughout the body assists in flushing fluids through the valves of the circulatory system and stimulates cell walls to become thicker and stronger. In addition, the body's oxygen consumption is measurably more efficient on a trampoline compared with running or jumping on a hard surface.

A good example of all-around biomechanical measurement is a device made by Stairmaster. It is a gravity-activated treadmill that simulates the climbing of steps. Walking up a flight of stairs uses some of the largest muscle groups in the body, and the total measurements give an excellent indication of one's general physical condition.

*Stairmaster unit in exercise spa.*

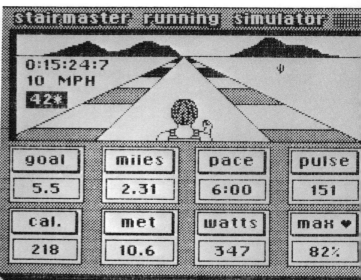

*Stairmaster video displays compute "floors climbed" or "miles run," time and speed, energy units used, and heart rate during exercise.*

The Stairmaster treadmill looks like a short section of an escalator. As you step up from one stair to the next, your weight pushes the steps down so that you remain in place. A brake lever allows the treadmill to turn more freely or with more resistance so you can regulate climbing speed and effort. The machine has both a video screen and a computer printout. The screen, placed so that you can watch it as you climb, shows the number of steps climbed per minute, kilometers you have traveled, the number of watts of power you have generated, your oxygen consumption, and the number of calories you have burned. A monitor cord attached to the tip of one finger also measures your pulse and electronically transfers it to the video display to show your heart rate. At the same time a computer printout summarizes all of the biomechanical information for permanent record.

Similar computer equipment ranging from simple electronic dials and digital displays to video screens and printouts now comes with many units of home exercise equipment or can be added on if desired. Such innovations make elements of biomechanical measurement available to both amateur and professional athletes alike.

## RESISTANCE TRAINING

Resistance training, using muscular strength against physical resistance, is one of the most basic forms of body conditioning. There are several common kinds, each employing different equipment.

The first is lifting free weights. This was popularized in the 1940s in the United States by Bob Hoffmann, a former head coach of the U.S. Weight Lifting Team. By the 1948 Olympics, a number of American athletes were advocates of weight training. Hoffmann founded the York Barbell company, and within a short time bodybuilder Joe Wieder founded his own company to compete with York. The sport of bodybuilding boomed, and today free weights can be purchased from many sources. Plates of specified weight are slipped over the ends of a metal bar and held in place by collars and clamps. Some weights are made of cast iron. Others are made of sand or concrete poured into plastic casings. There are now lifting bars of every conceivable length, size, and shape, with hand grips ranging from straight to curved to those shaped into loops with cross handles. All have some provision for adding and subtracting plate weights.

Free weights can be used alone or with an exercise bench. The basic type looks like a piano bench with a pad. A more flexible bench may have a section that inclines like the back of a lounge chair and fold-out wings with vertical poles and brackets to support the weight bar. More elaborate benches have a pivot unit at one end for exercising legs in various positions and an extension handle for doing arm and back exercises. Whatever the features of the bench, all of the resistance comes from adding or subtracting free weights. The weights come in stepped poundages. A typical set might consist of several 2½-lb. or 3-lb. weights, several 6-lb., 12½-lb., and 25-lb. weights, and perhaps even a few 50-lb. weights. It is best to start with a few basic sizes and add more as strength increases.

Free weights also come as barbells of fixed size and weight. The typical shape is of two slightly flattened balls with a gripping bar in between. However, since barbells are not adjustable, more of these are required than loose plates. The most complete sets usually are purchased by gyms, spas, or professional training facilities.

The action of lifting free weights is called *isotonic*, meaning "against constant resistance." Actually, any weight is lifted against the pull of gravity, which means that resistance depends on the angle of the moving body lever to the ground. If you are pushing a weight directly upward above your head in a "military press," the resistance of gravity is fairly constant. However, suppose you are doing arm curls in a standing position. At the start of the exercise your arms hang toward the floor. As you begin to flex your arms at the elbow, the bar and weights first swing horizontally away from your body and there is little lifting involved. But as your arms flex further, the weights begin to swing upward in an arc. Resistance of gravity increases and is greatest when your forearms are parallel to the ground. Then, as the bar continues to arc toward your shoulders, your forearms gradually come up into a vertical position, and once again there is less resistance. When you let the weight back down, the changes in resistance are the same but in reverse sequence. The poundage you can lift is limited to how much you can raise through the horizontal part of your arm flex. For this reason some extra trunk swing is usually added to assist the arm swing, or a partner can assist as needed, so that the lifter can work with heavier poundages.

A second type of resistance exercise was introduced in Germany in the early 1950s. Scientific studies there suggested that muscle strength could be developed faster and better by static contraction. The new method was called *isometric*, meaning "constant measure," and used no motion at all. Resistance was supplied by fixed supports or parts of the body itself. For instance, suppose you want to use an isometric exercise for the same muscles used in curling free weights. These would include the biceps area of the upper arm and the shoulder. Static resistance can be supplied by a desk or shelf built firmly against supporting walls. Place your hands under the edge of the shelf and try to lift it. Of course,

Left: *Curl with free weights.*

Right: *Isometric "curl" against fixed resistance. Both exercises strengthen biceps of upper arms.*

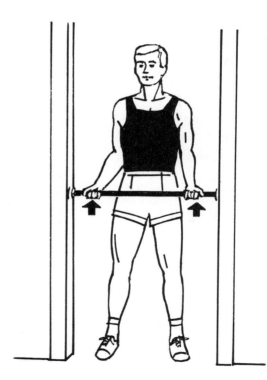

it stays in place, but your arm and shoulder muscles will contract as they did with the curl. Or suppose you wish to exercise the pectoral muscles across the chest. To do this isotonically with free weights, you would lie on an exercise bench on your back with arms extended out and down on either side, each hand holding a barbell. You would then raise your arms, locked in a slightly bent position, until the barbells came together above your chest. This exercise is called the butterfly, since it looks as if you are flapping your "wings."

With isometrics you can do a similar exercise using only your own body. In a vertical or horizontal position, extend slightly bent arms out in front of your chest, with the palms of your hands together. Now push your hands together as you keep your arms locked. You will feel the same pectoral muscles tighten across your chest that contracted during the butterfly with free weights.

One advantage of isometrics is that you can exert exactly as much effort as you choose. In a typical isometric you start with gradual pressure and then build up to maximum, holding the position for ten seconds. Even though there is no movement, muscle tissue contracts and the stimulation can produce both an increase in strength and sometimes in muscle size. Another advantage of isometrics is that they can be done anywhere with no special equipment. Disadvantages are that only one part of the range of motion is used, and flexibility is limited. Therefore, it is a good idea to combine isometrics with reaching, stretching,

Above: *Butterfly with free weights and arms bent.*

Below: *Isometric contraction with hands pressed together. Both exercises strengthen large pectoral muscles of chest.*

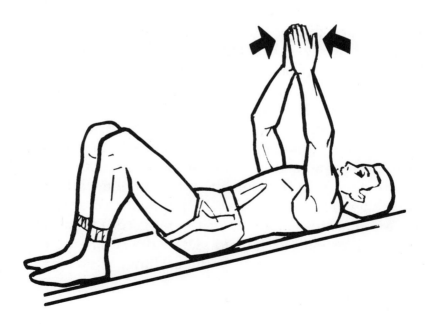

and flexing routines. Occasionally two people can do isometrics together, each one bracing or resisting the strength of the other. With this system it is easy to include positions that require both stretch and strength.

The newest form of resistance exercise is called *iso-kinetic*. This uses machines that offer the same kind of resistance as free weights but accommodate it no matter what position a body unit is in throughout its movement. Such machines usually operate by means of pressure cylinders. If the cylinders are filled with fluid, the system is *hydraulic*. If they are filled with air, the system is *pneumatic*. The cylinders work like a bicycle pump. As the pump handle is lowered, the air or liquid in the cylinder is compressed and offers resistance. If the handle is lowered slowly, resistance is slight. But if the handle is pushed down more rapidly, resistance increases in proportion to the force applied. Thus the resistance is constantly accommodated.

Here is how an isokinetic machine works. Suppose you intend to exercise the quadriceps muscles of your thigh. You sit on the end of a bench with one leg hanging over, flexed at the knee. Your shin fits against an adjustable pad on a pivot arm. As you straighten your leg, you feel an even amount of resistance through the entire motion. As you apply greater force, the resistance increases while speed remains the same. On some isokinetic machines, such as those made by Biodex and Chattex, the lever continues to offer resistance as

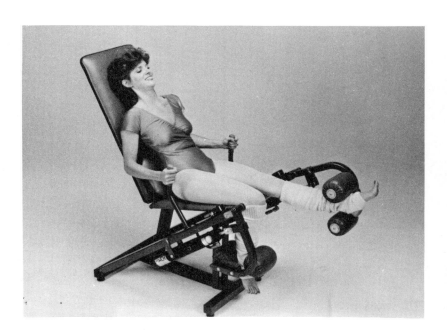

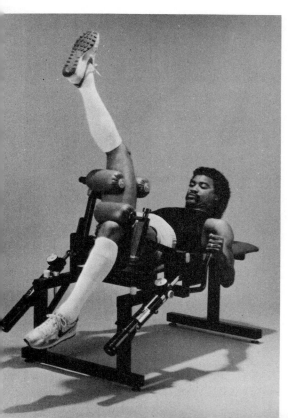

Omnitron by Hydrafitness provides reciprocal exercise, or resistance in opposing directions.

Above: *Quads and hamstrings.*

Left: *Hip flexors and hip extensors.*

Opposite left: *Biceps and triceps.*

Opposite right: *Chest and back.*

you lower your foot again, exactly as if you are continuing to hold a weight as you set it down slowly. With other machines, such as those by Cybex and Hydra-fitness, your ankle is held between two pads or clamped in a circular band. You still contract the quads on the top of your thigh to extend the leg, but on the way down you contract the hamstrings on the back of your thigh instead, to flex your leg and force the lever down. These machines provide reciprocal exercise, or alternation between opposing muscle groups.

On a few machines the exercise arm will move itself electromechanically at a preset speed or force, and you

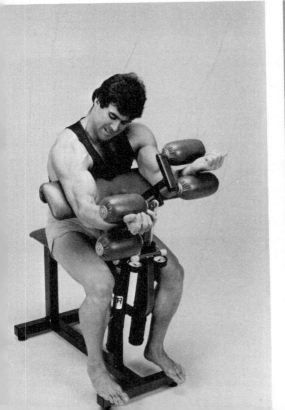
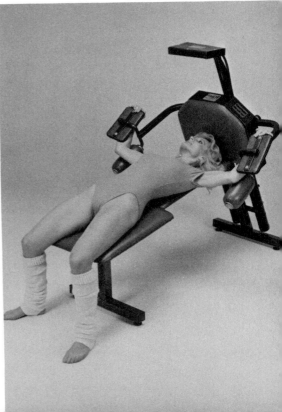

resist this force as you follow the motion of the arm. One machine with this feature is KinCom, manufactured by Chattex. It can be used for therapy or recovery from injury as well as for strength training.

Many of the newer machines in this category can be connected to computers providing digital or video displays and chart printouts with detailed information about power exerted, the work done over a period of time, the number of repetitions in a given time, and other measurements. Thus they are not only training devices but fitness and medical monitors as well.

Some exercise machines employ weights but are designed with safety features or with some of the features of isokinetic equipment. For example, handling

*Cybex II+ system for testing and exercising all major body joints offers control of acceleration, speed, range of motion, and computer data printout.*

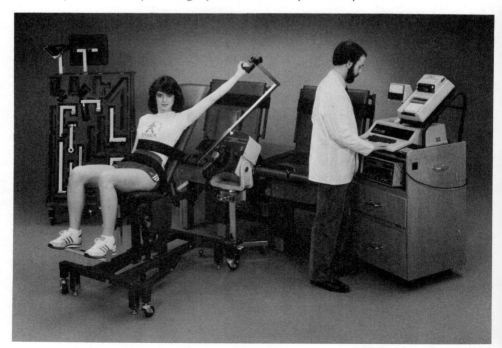

*Lee Haney, two-time heavyweight Mr. Olympia, does seated "military" presses on a Smith machine. Weights are guided up and down vertical poles and can be locked easily into safety catches by rotating wrists back slightly.*

free weights can be dangerous if the weights are dropped during a heavy lift. One improvement is to add guided channels for the weight bar. Such a design is the Power Safe rack, developed by Lou Reicke, the strength coach of the Pittsburgh Steelers football team. With this device special channels slide vertically on fixed pipes. Holes in the movable channels allow a horizontal bar to be inserted between them at any desired level. These vertical guides limit the path of the weight, reducing risk of strain or accident. Small permanent projections at the outer base of each channel allow free weights to be added as needed. Many other weight racks now offer similar safety features.

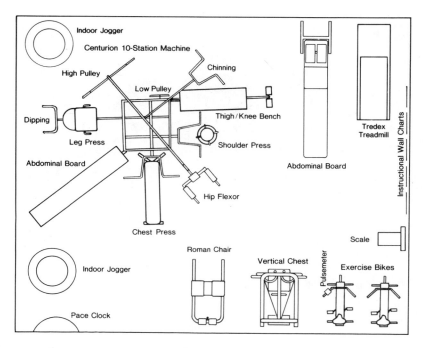

**Above:** *plan view of exercise room designed by Universal. Exercise bikes are used for warm-up. Indoor joggers (rebounders) can be used between stations to keep muscles warm.*

**Right:** *Universal 10-station machine with all stations in use.*

Other composite machines link hand grips or pivot handles to wires and pulleys so the weights can be stacked within channels of the pulley assembly, out of the way of the exercise movements. A popular example is the exercise complex with stations on every side made by Universal and found in many gyms and fitness centers. Several people can exercise at the same time, simply switching places at the various stations.

A variation of the weight and pulley principle appears in the equipment manufactured by Nautilus. This

is considered to be isotonic with variable resistance. With Nautilus each machine provides for only one or just a few precise exercise motions, and anywhere from eight to twelve machines are used for a complete work-out. On many of these machines the pulley wheels are designed as off-center cams that happen to have the irregular shape of a nautilus shell, giving the equip-

*Nautilus double shoulder machine.*
Left: *Arms are raised laterally to exercise deltoid muscles of the shoulders.* Right: *Overhead press exercises deltoids, upper sections of trapezius of the back, and triceps of the upper arms.*

**Above:** *Nautilus machine for both leg abduction (away from midline of body) and adduction (toward midline) exercises outer hips and inner thighs in an opposing set of motions.*

**Below:** *Nautilus biceps/triceps machine has independent stations for exercising triceps (arm extension) at left, and biceps (arm flexion) at right. Resistance is regulated by chains, cams, and stacked barbell plates.*

ment its name. When wrapping around the smallest radius of the cam, the cable is pulled a relatively short distance to displace the weight. However, when wrapping around the largest off-center radius of the cam, the cam itself rotates with the cable, and the weight must be raised a greater distance for the same cable displacement, increasing resistance. Thus resistance varies with the curve of the cam. To the person using the machine the full exercise movement feels smoother than lifting a free weight, and the effort seems more evenly distributed throughout the range of motion.

Studies comparing isotonic (free weights) and isokinetic training demonstrate that the greatest improvements in strength come from rapid isokinetic exercises with high resistance. Part of this effectiveness apparently comes from the fact that isokinetic machines allow maximum tension throughout the whole range of motion. Research also shows that greater benefit comes from the negative portion of a resistance motion. For instance, contracting a muscle to shorten it toward its center is called *concentric motion*. Extending the same tensed muscle against gravity or resistance is called *eccentric motion*. A muscle can support more resistance in this negative phase. The eccentric motion stimulates greater gains in strength and muscle size than the concentric motion of the same exercise.

Some isokinetic machines offer a speed range of from zero degrees to 200 to 300 degrees of motion per second. (Movement in a half circle would be 180 degrees). Thus an athlete in a sport that demands running, jumping, or throwing now can exercise body parts against resistance at speeds as great as, or sometimes greater than, those required by the particular sport. This way quickness is maintained or even improved as strength increases. The jumper extends height, the sprinter increases speed, and the overhand serve of the tennis player becomes faster and more powerful.

All forms of resistance training have their advantages and disadvantages, but the modern machines offer an excellent opportunity for exercising isolated muscle groups effectively and safely. A well-planned school, college, or pro sports gym will probably offer an array of devices and equipment including adjustable free weights, barbells, pulley or hydraulic resistance machines, pedal exercycles, and adjustable exercise benches. Workouts may consist of warm-ups on exercycles, then a circuit routine on a series of machines, interspersed with brief intervals of rest, jogging, or cycling. Cool-down should consist of decreased resistance exercise and stretching. Workouts sometimes are rounded out with a hot whirlpool bath for muscle relaxation, and perhaps a dry-heat sauna before a shower.

FREE EXERCISE
Some of the exercises that are the most fun are done with no equipment except your own body. They are called *free exercises* and range from body-weight resis-

tance movements to aerobics and stretches. Some of the most popular ones are described here. While these can serve as general examples, any personal exercise program should be undertaken on the recommendation of your own physician and with the guidance of an exercise specialist.

*Push-ups*

Push-ups exercise several upper body muscle groups, emphasizing triceps, deltoids, and pectorals. When they are done in proper form, the body is locked horizontally chiefly by muscles of the back, abdominals, hips, and the quadriceps that extend the legs. Thus push-ups provide an isotonic exercise for arms and chest and an isometric exercise for the lower body. Push-ups can be done slowly, rapidly, or with a fast push upward and a slower descent, bracing against gravity. If push-ups are too difficult, they should be done first with

*Push-ups, with back straight and hands below shoulders.*

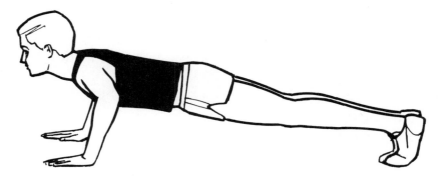

knees touching the floor until arm strength builds up. Or push-ups can be made more difficult by gradually elevating the feet above the head. A trained gymnast may be able to do what amounts to a push-up from a handstand on parallel bars or rings, requiring great upper body strength.

Push-ups can be done either with hands close together, directly under the shoulders, or with hands wide apart. Extra strength and flexibility can be gained by doing push-ups with hands on two low stools or other supports. In this way the upper body can dip lower than usual between the stools to flex the upper arms back at the shoulders. This version of push-ups is especially good for wrestlers as a means of preventing shoulder injury.

*Sit-ups*

Sit-ups is the standard exercise for the abdominal muscles. The most common method is done while lying with back flat on the floor and hands clasped behind the head. Legs should be flexed to avoid strain in pelvic muscles. Girls will probably keep their feet on the floor, since they have more body weight below the trunk. Boys may find that their legs pop into the air during the exercise. Although someone else can then hold the feet down, some exercise specialists recommend against this so that any strain on the lower back is avoided. As you raise your trunk, imagine that you are rolling your body up from your chest to your legs.

*Version of sit-ups that does not strain lower back. Stomach tightens and tucks as hands touch knees.*

When you reach a sitting position, immediately lower your trunk again smoothly so that your back touches the floor. But do not quite unwind all the way before starting to roll up again.

A common variation is to free the arms and extend them forward as a sitting position is reached, then to bring them back behind the head again as the trunk is lowered. Another style is to touch the right elbow to the left knee, and vice versa. The twisting motion of the trunk exercises the oblique muscles at either side of the abdominals and, like reaching for your toes, adds a useful stretch to the routine.

For those who are not used to doing regular sit-ups, the solution is half sit-ups, or "curl-ups," which are actually safer and can be just as effective. Start flat on your back with knees flexed, but instead of raising the entire trunk, barely begin to curl up so that only the shoulders are off the floor. Hold the abdominal muscles contracted for a few seconds before lowering the shoulders almost all the way and then tightening once more.

Sit-ups can be made more difficult by doing them on an incline plane with feet higher than the head. They also are done by serious bodybuilders in an upside-down position in which the legs are bent at the knees over a bar so that the upper body hangs free.

### Dips

The strength required for dips depends partly on body weight, and dips may be difficult at first. By starting with some variations they can be worked up to gradually. A good home arrangement is to use two firm chairs with backs facing each other about a foot and a half apart. For safety place the sides of the chairs against a wall. With arms locked, brace yourself between the chairs by clasping the backs of the chairs with your hands. Use small folded towels for padding if the grip is not comfortable. Slide your feet forward so that your legs are at a slight angle but feet are still flat on the floor. Now bend your arms to lower your trunk vertically between the chairs. Also flex your knees, and use your leg strength to assist your arms as much as needed. Dip as low as you can between the chair backs and then straighten your arms again.

As your arms get stronger with repeated practice, you can use your legs less until they do no work at all. Then you can graduate to dips between the seats of

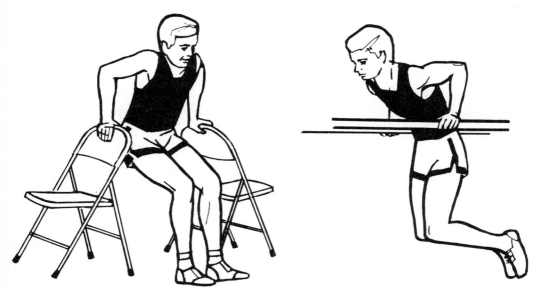

Left: "Easy" dips between carefully placed chairs, with legs assisting arms.

Right: Full-strength dips between parallel supports.

the chairs, with legs extended straight out, directly in front of you and heels resting on the floor. In this position your trunk is still upright. Your legs cannot help you, but part of their weight is removed from the exercise.

Now you are ready for free dips. You will probably need to use apparatus such as parallel bars or the dip handles on a Universal Gym or similar piece of equipment. Gripping the bars with arms bent, jump and raise yourself to full vertical position. Tuck your legs enough so that your toes will not touch the floor, and then lower yourself between the bars. When you extend your arms again, you will be lifting your full body weight.

Dips exercise large groups of upper body muscles, including the triceps of the upper arms, the pectorals of the chest, the broad latissimus dorsi muscles at either side of the back, and the front lobes of the deltoids. Doing free dips is an excellent upper body strength and body-building routine.

*Rope Climb*

Most gyms have a thick rope hanging from a rafter as a standard piece of equipment. A rope tied securely around a heavy branch of a large tree will work just as well. In doing the rope climb, it is easy to vary the style to suit your strength.

Start by pulling yourself up a short distance with both hands and quickly clamping the rope between your knees and the inside edges of your gym shoes, or by crossing your ankles with the rope wrapped between. Once you have decided on a secure foot lock, you can practice going up and down, first for short distances, then all the way to the top.

Next you can combine the foot lock with a style in which you reach up alternately with one hand at a time. Or if you have sufficient upper body strength, you may be able to use the professional style, in which your arms do all the work one by one as your legs hang completely free of the rope. Of course, when you reach the top of the climb, or when your arms become too

*Standard rope climb, with legs assisting arms.*

*Full-strength pull-ups with underhand grip.*

tired, you can use your feet to clamp and assist. The rope climb is excellent exercise for agility, upper body strength, and the muscles of the inner thigh.

*Pull-ups*

A pull-up is a means of hanging from a bar and using the arms to bring the head up to the level of the bar. There are several styles. The first two are really chin-ups since the body is raised so that the chin comes just above the level of the bar. One is the underhand chin in which the bar is gripped with palms facing you. The other is the overhand chin in which the hands are wrapped around the bar with palms facing away from you. Because of the twist in the wrist, the overhand version requires that hands be spaced farther apart in a wide grip. With an even wider grip you can do behind-the-neck pull-ups in which you tilt your head slightly down and pull your shoulders toward the bar until the back of the neck touches it.

To get the greatest benefit from pull-ups the movements must be smooth and complete. Without kicking or jerking your body, raise yourself all the way, lower yourself until your arms are straight, then immediately pull up again. You will feel the greatest work being done in the biceps of your upper arms. However, these are assisted by the upper parts of the pectorals of the chest, the latissimus dorsi muscles at the sides of the back, as well as sections of the deltoids. Overhand or reverse-grip chins use more of the latissimus dorsi muscles, and behind-the-neck pull-ups throw even more work to the back.

Depending on your size and body weight, pull-ups may be difficult at first. You can use a stool for assistance in the beginning. Place the stool facing you and about one foot in front of the overhead bar. Hang so that your toes are on the edge of the stool and your legs are flexed. If the stool is tall enough, you will be able to stand on it to some extent and use your legs to assist as you pull yourself up with your arms. As you practice and become stronger you can use your legs less until they are relaxing on the stool. Then you are strong enough to skip the stool and to do free-hanging pull-ups with your body weight. Pull-ups are excellent for developing upper body strength and appearance.

## AEROBICS

The word *aerobic* is closely associated with aerobic dancing, a type of free exercise that has become popular in the last decade. The person mainly responsible for this is Jacki Sorensen. As a youngster, Jacki was trained in ballet, modern dance, tap dancing, and acrobatics. Later, when she was married and her husband was in the Air Force, Jacki developed an exercise class for a television station at an overseas base. The inspiration was an Air Force program of aerobics de-

*Jacki Sorensen, pioneer in developing and promoting the popular fitness sport of aerobic dancing.*

veloped by Dr. Kenneth Cooper. Part of his program was a test for the mile-and-a-half run, with twelve minutes considered a good fitness time. Jacki choreographed a few routines for the television station, drawing on her dance background. The exercises were calculated to increase the heart rate and to promote cardiovascular fitness, in line with the goals of Dr. Cooper's program.

When Jacki moved to New Jersey in 1971, she started a similar aerobic dance class in the basement of a church. After three months she had twenty classes each week scattered around neighboring communities. Soon she began doing clinics for conventions. Interest spread, resulting in a business that she ran from her home after moving to California. Today thirty-seven states, Japan, and Australia all offer Jacki Sorensen aerobics classes.

The purpose of the aerobic exercises is to provide at least twenty minutes of conditioning to elevate heart rate within a natural and safe range. Over three thousand instructors have been trained to monitor heart rates and to administer *cardiopulmonary resuscitation*, or *CPR*. All instructors must run Dr. Cooper's twelve-minute mile-and-a-half twice each year. The popularity of Jacki Sorensen's aerobic dance has spawned numerous similar programs throughout the country. Although aerobic exercise programs initially attracted mainly girls and women, now many have been modified to appeal to coeducational groups.

Any fitness program, including either resistance

training or aerobic exercise, should both start and finish with warm-ups and stretches. Stretches allow the body to adapt gradually to muscular stress, increase the range of motion in body joints, and prevent injury. An additional benefit may be to reduce muscle soreness. Exercise physiologist Herbert deVries experimented with college students referred to him by coaches and trainers. He found that muscle pain was relieved by static stretching.

## STATIC STRETCHES

Static stretches are body positions that pull muscles and tendons to maximum length. When used regularly, stretches increase this resting length. The result is a more limber body that is not easily injured by the sudden demands of athletic competition. Here are three basic stretches. Others can be recommended for you by a qualified exercise physiologist or athletic trainer.

### Wall Push-up

Stand about two feet from a wall and facing it. Let yourself tip forward and cushion yourself with flexed arms so that your forehead touches the wall. Keep your back straight and your feet flat on the floor. Hold for ten seconds. Push yourself away from the wall and repeat. In the angled position the hamstrings at the back of your knees and especially the Achilles tendons at the back of your ankles are stretched. Gradually in-

crease the distance you stand from the wall to a maximum of about four feet.

### Toe Pull

Lie on your side with one arm extended alongside your head. Grab your bent leg at the ankle with your free arm. Pull your leg out and behind you. Hold this

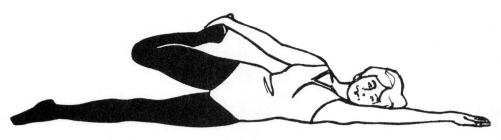

position for ten seconds. Repeat the stretch with the other arm and leg. This position lightly stretches the psoas muscles, which connect the upper leg to the pelvis, and also stretches the chest, upper arm, shin, and especially the quadriceps of the thigh.

### "Yoga" Stretch

Sit on the floor with one leg out straight and the other folded so that your foot is tucked against your inner thigh. Lean out over the straight leg with arms stretched and head down. Hold for ten seconds. Repeat with the other leg extended. With practice you can lean farther forward and bring your chest down until your forehead actually drops to your knee. This position stretches arms, neck, upper and lower back, hamstrings, and the muscles of the inner thigh.

Use these stretches both for warm-up and cool-down to increase flexibility and joint strength and to reduce the risk of injury.

# 4/Medicine and Psychology

SPORTS INJURIES

The most common sports injuries are to joints, including knees, ankles, feet, fingers, wrists, elbows, shoulders, and the neck and back. These are the parts of the body most subject to weight-bearing stress, twisting stress, or impact. Most injuries are minor, and it is the job of the team trainer to assist athletes with both prevention and treatment. Chronic or repeating injuries may be from overuse or from a biomechanical problem. When injuries are acute, or more severe, the services of a team physician are required. Typically an athletic trainer has a background in prevention, treatment, care, and rehabilitation of injury. However, expertise comes from long experience in treating athletes

101

and relying on those procedures that regularly prove most effective.

Fortunately many injuries respond to a simple formula of treatment, abbreviated by the word *RICE*. *R* stands for rest. *I* stands for ice. *C* stands for compression, and *E* stands for exercise. Suppose an athlete has sprained an ankle. The injury most likely involves stretching and minor tears in the connecting ligaments on either side of the ankle caused by the foot rolling on edge from being poorly placed, stressed, or twisted. Where there is physical trauma, body fluids flood into the area from surrounding tissues. The ankle will quickly swell and become painful as internal pressure increases.

Step one of RICE is to get the athlete off the injured foot to rest it. Then step two follows immediately. Ice cubes or an ice pack may be placed directly against the injured area for a limited time. (From fifteen to twenty minutes is frequently recommended.) Step three of RICE is to use compression. This is done with a compression wrap, and every trainer will have his or her own methods of wrapping the ankle quickly with an elastic bandage. The bandage can be applied directly over the ice pack. The ankle must be wrapped tightly enough to keep the swelling down but not so tightly as to cut off circulation. The bandage can be left in place for a short time until further medical treatment is available.

Once swelling is under control, perhaps within two to seven days, the medical doctor treating the injury

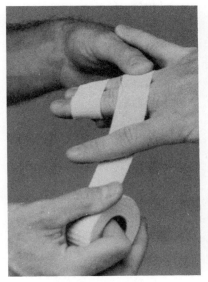

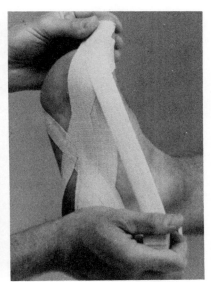

*Elastic tape can be used for finger straping, toe straping, and arch support.*

may recommend applying heat to aid healing. A heating pad can be wrapped around the ankle, or the ankle can be soaked in warm water. Once healing has begun, the ankle can be tested by being moved carefully. As soon as the foot can bear weight without unusual pain, it is ready for exercise, the last step of RICE. Moderate walking and massage will be beneficial. As a rule, the ankle will recover more quickly if it is encouraged to carry out its usual functions as soon as possible.

Minor injuries, bruises, and sprains that occur to other body joints, such as knees, elbows, and wrists can usually be treated successfully with the same formula. However, today there are ways of both preventing such injuries and improving recovery. A joint that has been injured once may remain susceptible to reinjury.

Of course, the best solution is a long-term program of exercise therapy to strengthen the muscles, tendons, and ligaments involved. But one immediate precaution is to tape the area during hard training or competition. This restricts motion slightly, keeps parts in place, and provides a cushion against impact.

A greater precaution is to use a limited-motion brace, and several unique types have been developed. For example, Aircast makes a special bandage for an injury called "tennis elbow" that occurs with tennis players, baseball players, football quarterbacks, and others who use the arm with a whipping motion. Such movements easily strain muscles on the outside of the forearm just below the elbow, causing stretch or tearing injury to the muscle tendon. The Aircast device includes a stretch bandage and a small, air-filled plastic cushion beneath it that presses directly against the strained muscle, reducing the tendency to new injury.

*Air cushion units by Aircast, including "tennis elbow" guard and inflatable knee and ankle braces to permit controlled motion.*

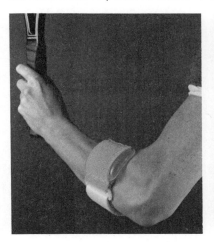
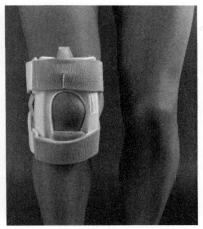

An ankle brace using the same principle is made of two sections of curved plastic that connect beneath the arch of the foot. Within each section is a long plastic bag that is inflated by mouth to the desired air pressure. The unit is fastened around the lower leg and ankle with Velcro straps. It acts as a compression device to limit swelling. At the same time normal muscle contractions cause a "milking" action to massage the injured area, aiding circulation and speeding healing. The ankle device also restricts excessive motion while allowing the foot to fit in a shoe. Experiments with basketball players show that with the brace on, an athlete can immediately play again with safety on a moderately sprained ankle. Wearing the brace while exercising cuts down on the aftereffects of the injury and shortens recovery time. Actually, there are various similar devices available for ankle bracing, and methods are constantly being improved.

Many injuries to feet, ankles, and knees come from wearing improper shoes. Any athletic shoe must be both supportive and flexible, snug but not cramped, with about the width of a thumb between the big toe and the tip of the shoe. A running shoe must be low-cut with a flexible sole. The sides of a basketball shoe should be high and firm enough to help control excessive side-to-side flexion of the ankle. There should be ample cushion for the sole of the foot, preferably including a soft arch support. Individual prescription inserts, or *orthotics*, are now used by many athletes for correction of foot and gait abnormalities, prevention of injury, and improved performance.

When injuries occur to the neck or back, it is extremely important not to aggravate the damage. It is possible to cause complete paralysis of the spine just by moving the injured person before proper diagnosis is made. Such a judgment should be made by a medical doctor on call, or the regularly assigned team physician.

Many improvements have been made in the protective clothing worn by athletes in contact sports, including light weight pads and shields and designs that allow quick access in case of injury. A good example is the modern football helmet with an inner shock-absorbing lining separated from the protective plastic shell. The innovation of the face mask has prevented many injuries to nose and eyes, although the mask is sometimes grabbed illegally by a tackler, which then can cause a violent wrench to the neck. If a player is down on the field and a neck injury is suspected, it is best to temporarily leave on both the shoulder pads and helmet to keep injured parts from shifting further until professional medical help arrives.

One modern development that has raised new issues of sports safety is artificial turf, a substitute for the natural grass fields that prevent dust and erosion and provide an ideal cushioned surface for many sports. The idea began in 1965 as a solution to a problem in

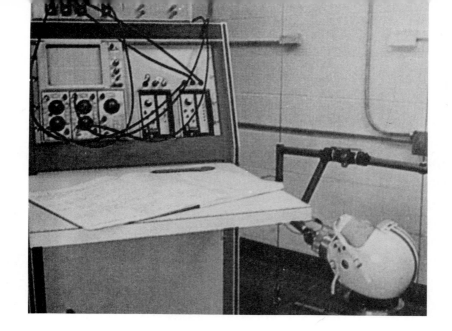

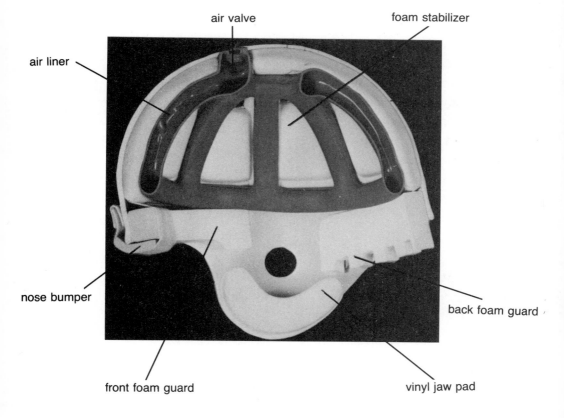

air valve

foam stabilizer

air liner

nose bumper

back foam guard

front foam guard

vinyl jaw pad

Opposite above: *Bike football helmet is scientifically tested for shock absorption.*

Opposite below: *Bike IV junior-high football helmet includes APS plastic shell, molded foam liner, air-inflated inner liner, nose bumper, back and front cushions, and vinyl jaw pads.*

Above: *Football protective wear includes helmet with face mask, shoulder pads, rib protector, air-foam biceps pads, hip pads, thigh pads, elbow pads, knee and shin pads, hand gloves, and elastic tape.*

the Astrodome, which covers the baseball field of the Astros in Houston, Texas. The new dome kept out the weather and allowed light to enter but not enough to maintain the grass field. Monsanto Chemical Company was asked to cover the baseball infield with an experimental artificial turf. It looked good and stayed in place. It was possible to play on it, although balls bounced in a more lively way and with a spin that was not characteristic of grass.

The following year the entire floor of the Astrodome was carpeted with artificial grass. First intended only for indoor use, the product soon was adapted to outdoor fields as well. Baseball fields, then football fields, and even soccer fields were converted to the new turf. A typical problem with natural grass fields was seasonal growth. Particularly in temperate zones, the months for playing football coincided with those in which grass tended to die off. Furthermore, heavy rains could turn playing fields to slippery lakes of mud that were difficult to dry off or repair. To accomplish the needed drainage with artificial turf, each field required a complete engineering production. First water-collection pipes were laid in gravel. These were covered with a second layer of gravel. Over this went a special layer of asphalt through which water could penetrate. Then came the artificial turf, which consisted of a perforated rubber pad under a carpet of nylon strands twisted and anchored together.

A well-designed artificial field drains better than a

grass field, and the problems of mud and dying grass were eliminated. However a new set of problems replaced the old. The artificial turf would sometimes hump or buckle. Seams could open up or tear loose. While the added traction was more consistent than grass and enabled football running backs to cut and change direction without slipping, there was a price to pay. Feet literally "stuck" to the turf. Ankles were more easily twisted, and toes were jammed forward in shoes that would not slip along with the foot inside. The rough texture of the nylon grass acted like sandpaper on bare hands, arms, and legs, causing ugly abrasions that healed slowly and were very prone to infection. Even covered body parts became victims of the surface. Helmets and shoulder pads were gripped suddenly when contact was made with the turf, jarring the very muscles, tendons, and bones that they were designed to protect.

As early as 1971, Stanford Research Institute in California completed a six-year study of injuries among players in the National Football League. Seventeen body areas were considered: head, face, teeth, neck, shoulders, arms, elbows, wrists, hands, fingers, chest, feet, toes, back, hips, ankles, and knees. The study showed that in all seventeen categories natural grass was safer to play on than artificial turf. In 1978, SRI made another survey, this time of 1000 NFL players. Eighty-three percent preferred natural grass to artificial grass.

The NFL Players Association conducted its own injury studies and found that compared with grass, most turf injuries took longer to heal, the number of players placed on the injured reserve list increased by one third, and twice as many games were missed when injuries occurred on artificial surfaces. Among colleges the reports are similar. Recently the National Collegiate Athletic Association hired a research coordinator who studied the injuries of 750,000 players in 50 schools. The report showed that the rate of injury is around 50 percent higher on artificial turf than on natural grass.

One drawback to artificial turf that increases the chance of injury is its temperature response. Grass has a natural capacity to cool itself. Nylon grass, on the other hand, stores heat. Its temperature may be thirty degrees higher than the air three feet above the playing field. Some artificial fields become hot enough to actually fry an egg. Such heat destroys shoes and drains the energy of players who are literally dancing on a frying pan.

Turf injuries have stimulated the use of additional protective gear. For example, football players more frequently wear arm guards and special hand or palm gloves to avoid abrasive skin injuries. But at present the overall problem of increased artificial turf injuries has not been solved.

The rising need for research into sports safety, injury prevention, and treatment has given impetus to the new specialty of sports medicine. Team physicians and trainers are now a basic ingredient of almost any sports program from high schools through colleges and professional teams. At the same time specialized clinics have sprung up throughout the country.

An example of a modern sports medical facility is the Institute for Medicine in Sports, associated with Hamilton Hospital in central New Jersey. The Institute roster includes two orthopedic surgeons, a cardiologist, a podiatrist specializing in biomechanics and lower limb problems, a general practitioner, an athletic trainer, physical therapists, exercise physiologists, and a psychologist. Total facilities include an exercise and therapy room with resistance machines and computer monitoring equipment, a separate room for cardiovascular monitoring and therapy, and advanced digital equipment for measuring foot and leg motions.

A number of colleges are beginning to offer a basic four-year degree in sports medicine, and many national organizations now concentrate all or part of their activities on questions of sports fitness, medicine, and safety. These include the United States Olympic Committee, The American Academy of Sports Physicians, The American College of Sports Medicine, the American Academy of Podiatric Sports Medicine, the American Orthopaedic Society for Sports Medicine, and the President's Council on Physical Fitness and Sports. A worldwide organization, the International Federation of Sports Medicine, meets every two years as the Inter-

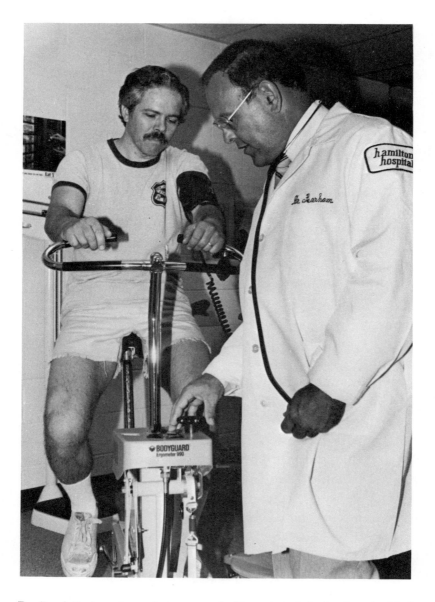

*Dr. Frank Barham demonstrates exercycle fitness test at the Institute for Medicine in Sports in Hamilton Square, New Jersey.*

national Congress and also every four years at the times of the Olympic Games to evaluate developments and to promote new scientific research.

## SPORTS SURGERY

In most sports the legs are the most stressed body parts, and the knees are the most frequently injured parts of the legs. The knee not only joins lower leg and thigh in rapidly changing angles, but it is expected to act as a shock absorber, receiving impact every time the foot strikes the ground. In addition, it is subject to rotating and twisting stresses in sports like volleyball, tennis, and basketball. In contact sports such as soccer, hockey, and football, the knee receives direct damage from collisions with other players, as well as falls on surfaces ranging from grass and clay to asphalt and artificial turf. It is no wonder the knee is so vulnerable.

Knee injuries range from mild muscle pulls or stretched tendons to torn and ruptured cartilages, ligaments, and splintered bone fragments. A single serious knee injury can take an athlete out of play for an entire season, or force an early end to a promising career.

A decade ago any knee surgery was a difficult procedure involving deep incisions, the stress of moving ligaments and tendons to gain access, and healing times of from eight to ten weeks. This has changed with the introduction of arthroscopic surgery. Fiberoptics—using flexible strands of glass to transmit intense light sources—has made possible a new medical instrument called the *arthroscope. Arthro* means "joint," and *scope* means "to view." An instrument no more than three to five milimeters wide is inserted into a body joint through a narrow incision, and the miniature light and lens system creates an image in an eyepiece attached to the outside end of the tube. Use of the instrument as an aid to surgery was pioneered in Japan in the first quarter of the twentieth century, and it was introduced in the West in the 1970s. Part of the popularity of arthroscopic surgery came with the development of microsurgical instruments to make the technique practical.

*Light source, fiberoptic cable, arthroscope, and microsurgical instruments by Zimmer.*

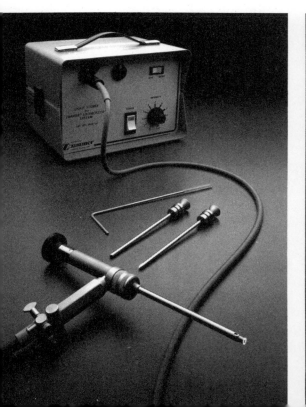
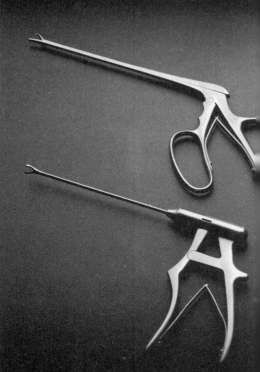

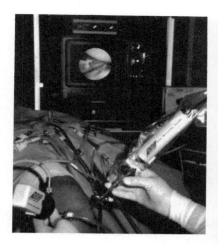

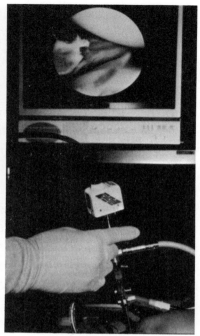

Video cameras for arthroscopic surgery include both vacuum tube and smaller solid-state models. Image of interior of knee is projected on high-resolution video screen.

A typical modern arthroscope combines two procedures in one. The surgical site must be cleansed with a sterile solution. Inside the viewing tube is a hollow outer sheath that carries a constant stream of sterile water. Within this cylinder are the fiberoptic light cables and a miniature telescopic lens system to view where the cable penetrates. Usually a tiny color TV camera is attached to the end of the tube, and a magnified image is projected on a video screen. The resolution of camera and screen can now be up to 300 lines per inch, finer than on a home TV set, and capable of producing an amazingly realistic and detailed picture.

The greatest application of the arthroscope is for knee surgery. The viewing tube passes through a small incision. A second incision allows a hollow tube, or *shunt*,

to be introduced to drain off the incoming sterile solution. And a third incision is made so that the tiny
surgical tools can be inserted. Narrow instruments for
slicing, cutting, and scraping can be slipped through a
thin, protective sheath. Or an electrically driven rotary
surgical blade can be inserted and controlled from outside the incision. To the surgeon, using the viewing
scope and surgical tool together feels like manipulating
the joysticks of a video game. When a local anesthetic
is used for the arthroscopic procedure, the patient may
actually be able to walk back to his or her room after
surgery.

An example of what arthroscopic surgery can accomplish is marathon runner Joan Benoit. This world
record holder underwent arthroscopic surgery on her
injured right knee. Seventeen days later she was
fit enough to win the marathon trial for the 1984
Olympics.

## DRUGS

Sports medicine must now deal with another trend that
threatens the health of athletes of all ages. Besides foods
and vitamins that are part of basic nutrition, there are
now chemical substances that imitate those produced
inside the body and can affect the body in specific ways.
These are the drugs, and their use in sports has created both controversy and tragedy. Naturally athletes
want to turn in peak performances, and it is tempting

to use artificial means to boost alertness or strength. Sometimes synthetic chemicals do accomplish these things. More often the benefits are doubtful, while the harmful side effects to body and personality can be devastating.

The most popular drugs are the *stimulants*, those that trigger nerve impulses and muscle firing to bring a feeling of being awake and "hyped." The most common are the *amphetamines*, usually called *uppers*. Amphetamines mask pain, and while they do not reduce fatigue, they create this illusion to the user. Amphetamines may remove some of the fear of performance, but they do not actually increase ability or strength. The athlete on amphetamines may believe he or she is performing well, when in fact the athlete is performing poorly and is risking permanent damage from untreated injuries. Athletes on amphetamines take longer to recover from endurance events. Furthermore, there are severe mood swings from high to low as the effect of the drug wears off. Taking amphetamines regularly becomes habit-forming, and the pattern is hard to break.

Another stimulant sometimes used by athletes is *cocaine*, a powder derived from the leaves of the tropical coca plant. Cocaine is partly an anesthetic. It blocks nerve impulses, bringing numbness to parts of the body. It also stimulates the central nervous system to speed heartbeat and breathing. Thus it imitates the body's response to fear or challenge.

However, the initial high from cocaine changes first to depression, then hallucination, and finally to a state resembling the mental illness called *schizophrenia*. The drug is addictive, and most users become habitually depressed or anxious. A very few people are extremely allergic to the drug, and for them almost any dosage can be fatal.

A growing list of professional athletes have been forced to admit that they could not control their use of cocaine and have entered treatment programs. A few have been arrested for passing the illegal drug. Some careers have been salvaged. Others have been ruined, either from physical or psychological damage or from the negative publicity accompanying involvement with cocaine.

Another group of chemicals used in sports are the *steroids*. One in common use is a drug called *cortisone*, which reduces inflammation and is normally taken on a prescription basis. Another type of steroid is called *anabolic*. Anabolic steroids are present naturally in a healthy body and help to heal damaged tissues. Synthesized in 1935 as derivatives of the male hormone testosterone, anabolic steroids first were administered to people who, because of illness or injury, could not produce their own naturally. Soon it was discovered that artificial steroids seemed to help athletes to gain strength, weight, and muscle size. First widely used by Soviet weight lifters, steroids were introduced in

Western countries in the 1950s. Research suggests that the main effect of steroids is to reduce fatigue so that training sessions can include more work. Those benefiting most from steroids in terms of muscular strength and size are athletes who push their training routines to the maximum with heavy resistance, such as body builders, Olympic weight lifters, shot-putters, or football players.

Ingested or injected steroids decrease the body's production of natural testosterone and become a substitute for the male sex hormone. When steroids are used by women athletes, they become more masculine in body build and power. Voices may become lower, and permanent facial hair may appear. Nevertheless, the regular use of steroids has been prominent in Eastern Bloc countries and is one reason that East German women became dominant in Olympic swimming events.

Research on steroids conflicts. There appear to be certain benefits; however, prolonged use can damage the heart, liver, kidneys, endocrine glands, and sex glands, even causing sterility in males. Steroids can cause parts of bone and joint units to harden prematurely, stopping growth before the body is fully developed.

One example of the extreme effects of steroids has been reported by Steve Courson, offensive guard for the Tampa Bay Buccaneers professional football team.

At age eighteen Courson already was a successful athlete, but like many football players he felt he had to push harder to compete. Courson started using steroids the summer before his sophomore year at South Carolina. Later he used steroids again during certain off seasons of his professional football career. One problem of steroid use has been the lack of conclusive information on how frequently steroids can be taken and what dosages may be safe. At one time Courson went on a crash program, taking one five-milligram steroid pill every day for thirty days in a row. He gained weight rapidly, and his muscular strength increased so much that by the end of the thirty days he could bench-press seventy-five pounds more than usual.

Steve felt dependent on the steroids, but the fact that they boosted his strength and performance on the playing field seemed worth the risk. Like other football players, he was monitored regularly for physical condition. One day he had a routine measurement of his heart rate. It was 160 beats per minute in the resting state, more than double the normal rate, and his heart was actually quivering in a dangerous state called *atrial fibrillation*. Amazingly, Steve was entirely unaware of his abnormal heart activity.

Because his life was threatened, Steve Courson stopped all use of steroids and publicly disclosed his story. He described dependency on the steroids as similar to that caused by drugs like cocaine. He said that heavy use of the steroids had turned him into "some chemically created clone of destruction."

After going off steroids, Courson's body weight dropped to the former level, and his bench press dropped by the same seventy-five pounds by which it had increased. His heart activity returned to normal. He continued to work out as vigorously as before, aware that he had lost a slight physical advantage against other football linesmen who may have boosted their strength with steroids. However, with Steve Courson, the decision to discontinue steroids was literally a lifesaver.

In the fall of 1984, a scandal involving the distribution of steroids broke at Clemson University. It began when a gifted member of the track team was found dead in his dormitory bunk. The runner was Augustinius Jaspers, who had competed for the Netherlands in the Summer Olympic Games in Los Angeles and later attended Clemson. An inquiry showed that Jaspers had been using an anti-inflamation drug called *phenylbutazone,* or *bute,* which he had obtained without a prescription. Further investigation uncovered a drug-traffic network in which steroids were regularly distributed and sold to male and female athletes in sports ranging from football to track and cross-country at both Clemson and Vanderbilt University. Dispensing such drugs without a doctor's prescription is illegal in most states, and those involved in the drug distribution were liable for criminal prosecution. Similar investigations were begun in other sections of the United States in an effort to put a stop to the damaging effects of the unauthorized distribution and use of anabolic steroids and other drugs.

Another controversial question of body chemistry revolves around a method of boosting the number of red cells in the blood. In 1972, Dr. Björn Ekblom of the Institute of Gymnastics and Sports in Stockholm, Sweden, was studying the storage of oxygen in the blood. As an experiment he had taken a quart of blood from each of four volunteers. The red blood cells, those that transport oxygen, were separated out and stored under refrigeration. One month later the red cells of each volunteer were replaced by transfusion. In the meantime the body had quickly replaced the missing red cells, and putting back the old ones amounted to "doubling up" on the number of red cells in the bloodstream. According to Dr. Ekblom, the oxygen-carrying capacity of the volunteers had been increased so that they could run longer distances or times on a treadmill before becoming exhausted. The idea attracted attention, and later, in 1980, at Old Dominion University's Human Performance Laboratory in Norfolk, Virginia, it was tested with twelve runners. The U.S. test showed that eleven of the twelve athletes ran better times after doubling up on red cells.

Since that time the procedure has come to be called *blood doping, blood boosting,* or probably more accurately, *blood packing*. The question raised is: Is it safe or even legal for an athlete to be infused with extra, stored red blood cells, or does this amount to introducing a foreign substance such as drugs or steroids?

The United States Olympic Committee policy prohibits "any physiological substance taken in abnormal quantity or taken by abnormal route of entry into the body, with the sole intention of increasing in an artificial and unfair manner performance in competition. . . ." This policy had been set up with drugs in mind and left the question somewhat open as to whether a person's own blood was something artificial.

The matter came to a head following the 1984 Summer Olympics when it was learned that seven members of the United States cycling team, including Steve Hegg, who had won both a gold and silver medal, had used blood doping just before the competition. One athlete had been boosted with his own red blood cells. However, the rest had received red cell transfusions from the blood of relatives or others with the same blood types. Physicians warned of the risks of infection involved in cross-matching blood, and the U.S. Olympic Committee issued a new statement that blood packing or doping was considered unacceptable under any conditions.

Regulation of artificial means of tampering with body chemistry has become more stringent as concern for safety increases. Today about twenty colleges test their football players for steroid use. The National Basketball Association has instituted a new antidrug program under which clubs assist players who volunteer for treatment, but a player may be banned from the NBA for failing a drug test based on the recommendation of an independent expert. Within the last two years The International Olympic Committee has instituted a blood analysis system that tests for the presence of more than 300 prohibited substances in the body, including steroids. In the Pan American Games in Venezuela, eleven world-class weight lifters were expelled from competition, and in 1984, all of the athletes competing in the summer Olympic Games were tested using the new procedures in the nearby laboratories of the University of California at Los Angeles.

Many athletes now shun artificial stimulants, realizing that the physical condition required for excellent competition can be achieved naturally through proper training. The athlete who is fit and is drug-free will be in top form for his or her event and will be using the body's natural balance of chemicals stimulated by the brain to achieve peak performance.

SPORTS PSYCHOLOGY

One of the newest areas of sports medicine is sports psychology. Psychologists, those who study mind and behavior, now work with coaches, trainers, and with athletes on a one-to-one basis to improve performance. There always have been a few athletes with exceptional natural motivation that enables them to outperform those with superior talent. But usually, just as each athlete has his or her own set of physical gifts and problems, so each has his or her own set of psychological strong points or weaknesses.

The athlete who excels at a particular sport sometimes has a unique experience on a day of peak performance. In this instance the movements of the game become so automatic that no conscious thought is given to them. Focus is so keen that the senses seem aware of what is happening everywhere at once. Objects become magnified or seem to travel in slow motion. For example, the batter at the plate seems to see the baseball coming toward him more slowly than it really is, and the ball looks so enlarged that even the seams are visible.

The feeling is almost of being in a trance, and the athlete cannot recall later what he or she was doing or thinking at the time. Psychologists use the term *flow* to describe this ideal state of mind and body. Apparently, flow is the complete coordination of an athletic activity on such a high level that problems like minor injury, fatigue, fear, or self-doubt are ignored. Oddly, the sense of self also disappears. The athlete is not doing something but is simply a part of the event itself.

An experience like that of flow often has been reported by long-distance runners or those who jog for exercise. At first there is an awareness of the effort the body is putting into the exercise: the muscle tensions, the impact of the feet, and the labor of breathing. But after going far enough, the runner reaches a point where the motions become more automatic and effortless. The usual aches may disappear, and there may be a feeling of euphoria, as if one could run forever.

Part of this probably comes from the "second wind," the adjustment of the body to increased heart rate, deeper breathing, and sustained requirements for more oxygen to be delivered to the muscles. But psychologists have learned that there is an additional benefit from extended exercise. The brain releases increased amounts of *endorphins*. These chemicals are the body's natural painkillers. When they are present in higher than the usual amounts, a person feels physically and emotionally "high."

The goal of psychological training is to habitually reach the ideal state of mind and body associated with certain times and activities. There are several ways to accomplish this. All of them involve heightened self-awareness, a process of getting in touch with inner thoughts, body parts and functions, and combining them into a more coordinated whole.

One technique is *visualization*, or *imaging*. The athlete sits quietly with eyes closed and mentally pictures an athletic activity from start to finish. For example, a pole vaulter would picture himself balancing the fiber glass pole at the end of the runway, leaning forward, then running down the track, feeling each step smoothly pounding faster and faster as the pole floats easily at his side. Then he would picture himself planting the pole accurately in the slanted box and imagine the jump and the pull, feeling the flexible spring of the pole, the twist of his body, and the pointing of the toes toward the crossbar. Everything is planned and rehearsed mentally in advance, and the visualized goal is always successful.

Visualization accomplishes several things at once. The sections of the brain and nervous system that coordinate movements are rehearsed and programmed in advance. And since in the mental exercise there are no errors, technique actually can be improved and a positive habit reinforced.

Visualization has been used by high-jumper Dwight Stones, a frequent record holder and participant in the 1984 Olympic Games. As the televised games focused on the high-jump competitions, the camera clearly showed Stones visualizing his moves before each jump. His eyes were fixed on the bar and his head bobbed slightly, then lifted as he visualized each step up to the high-jump stand, then the takeoff and the arch of his back over the crossbar.

Various relaxation techniques are also beneficial to athletes. For muscles to recover from training or competition, they must be able to relax completely. And

*World-class pole-vaulter Mike Tully.*

even during the stress of an event muscles shift the work load from group to group. When one part of the body is active, another part may be inactive. For example, if only one arm is required to move, it is a waste of effort for the other arm to become tense.

One relaxation technique is meditation. This is an emptying-out process in which the mind is freed of the usual associations that bring stress and tension. There are many styles of meditation, but one popularized by physician and author Dr. Herbert Benson is called the *relaxation response*. The idea is to mentally repeat a simple word such as *one*. This is done over and over again in a monotonous way along with each exhalation of breath. As the routine is repeated with regular sessions, it becomes easier for the mind to let go of its usual effort, and there is an accompanying change in body metabolism. Breathing and heart rate slow down, blood sugar drops, and muscular tension is reduced.

Another useful technique has been developed by biofeedback psychologist Dr. Lester Fehmi. Biofeedback is a means of monitoring inner body processes such as heart rate, temperature, sweating, muscular tension, or brain waves. This information is converted into signals such as lights or sounds. The feedback enables a person to learn to change or control these inner functions in a positive way.

In his clinic in Princeton, New Jersey, Dr. Fehmi combines biofeedback routines with his own method of relaxation, called OPEN FOCUS®. To use this approach, a person first listens to the voice of the psychologist offering suggestions for imagining spaces inside body sections and muscles and even imagining space surrounding the body. Statements are made, such as, "Can you imagine the space inside your ears?" or "Can you imagine the space inside your lungs?" Focusing attention both on the parts of the body and on the image of space brings relaxation and a synchronization of body systems similar to that induced by meditation. Subjects who practice OPEN FOCUS techniques are then better prepared to use special biofeedback routines to learn to monitor and control various body processes.

An example of these techniques in action came in 1979 when Dr. Fehmi was commissioned by the U.S. Olympic Committee to conduct sessions with twenty-two world-class male long- and middle-distance runners, including Mark Belger, Don Paige, and Steve Scott. Larry Ellis, head track coach at Princeton University, helped to initiate the project. The clinic ran for three days. It included OPEN FOCUS training plus biofeedback routines monitoring brain waves, muscle tension, sweat gland activity, and body temperature. For example, the brain-wave feedback used tones that indicated when alpha waves were generated. Alpha waves are those occurring between 8 and 13 times per second and are typical of a relaxed, but alert, state of mind

*800-meter runner Mark Belger receives biofeedback instruction from researcher Dr. Lester Fehmi.*

and body. Meters showed reductions in sweating and muscle tension or increases of hand temperature also associated with a beneficial state.

Dr. Fehmi reported that the Olympic athletes were excellent subjects. They compared OPEN FOCUS training to positive experiences of coordination, or flow, that they had noticed during training and competition. Most of the athletes easily could sense their own muscular tension, but at the same time most had little awareness of other body systems. Many had cold and sweaty hands before biofeedback training, which is characteristic of a stress response.

One biofeedback measurement that has proved most useful to athletes is that of muscle tension. This is called *electromyography,* or *EMG* for short. "Myo" means muscle in Greek and electromyography refers to the way of recording muscle activity electrically. When a nerve cell stimulates a muscle cell to fire, a small electric charge is produced. An electrode pasted or taped to the surface of the body will pick up electrical activity from the muscle or muscles nearest that location.

Suppose the EMG subject is a ski-jumper complaining of an annoying ache in the shoulders that gets worse on days of competition. Training films show that this athlete tends to hunch his shoulders very high just before he springs off at the end of the ramp.

In the lab a biofeedback trainer tapes a sensor at each side of the jumper's neck halfway between the neck and shoulders. The sensors are located on the upper slopes of the large trapezius muscle that raises the shoulders when the upper sections contract. Wires lead from the sensors to equipment that will translate small bursts of electrical activity into clicks that can be heard through a loudspeaker.

As the athlete relaxes in a chair, some clicks are heard on the speaker. Now the trainer asks the athlete to imagine preparing for his jump, pushing out onto the ramp, and holding his tuck position. The clicking sound gradually increases and becomes almost a blur at the moment the athlete thinks of stretching out at the end of the ramp. The neck muscles have become extremely tense at exactly this point in the sequence, a waste of the energy that is needed mainly in the legs and back.

The athlete is allowed to spend some time alone with the muscle biofeedback setup. He notices the times when there are fewer clicks than usual. These show when his neck muscles are naturally more relaxed. A calendar schedule is set up so that he can come in several times a week to practice the relaxation technique. With feedback training he learns to identify the relaxed feeling and to create it at will. Later, when actually practicing his ski jump, he is delighted to find that his shoulders no longer ache. The relaxation has become a habit. Thus biofeedback and visualization have combined to give the athlete a more effective way of improving performance.

Actually biofeedback is a form of biomechanics that can be used not only by psychologists but also by physiologists, therapists, surgeons, coaches, sports trainers, and others. In fact, a sophisticated form of electromyography is used at the research facilities of the U.S. Olympic Committee at Colorado Springs. Instead of a network of wires connecting sensors to monitors, each sensor is a tiny transmitter capable of broadcasting a signal up to 250 feet from its location. Thus an athlete can perform a normal range of body movements while muscle signals are collected by a receiving monitor and stored digitally for analysis.

The disciplines of medicine and computer science overlap to contribute to each other. In ways such as this, sports science has become a combination approach. Physical training, skills training, biomechanics, sports psychology, and medical therapy and rehabilitation all unite to provide the athlete with a total mind-body approach to fitness and performance. Athletes are better trained and conditioned than ever before, and there is more cooperation among coaches, trainers, physiologists, laboratory scientists, and members of the medical professions in sharing new knowledge and putting new techniques into practice. A scientific revolution has taken place and is still taking place in the understanding of the human body and its capacities for growth, strength, agility, control, and physical endurance. Whether the emphasis is on recreation or on professional achievement, today is the era of modern sports science.

# Glossary

*acceleration:* change in velocity divided by the time over which it occurs

*calorie (kilocalorie):* heat required to raise one kilogram of water one degree Centigrade

*centrifugal force:* force acting outwardly from a center

*centripetal force:* force acting inwardly toward a center

*force:* quantity necessary to accelerate a mass

*fulcrum:* pivot point of a lever

*G-force:* unit of force exerted by gravity on a body at rest

*kilogram:* unit of mass

*lever:* rigid rod rotated around a fulcrum

*MET:* metabolic equivalent; basic unit of oxygen consumed by the body at rest *momentum:* tendency of a moving object to continue its displacement

*power:* ability to move a mass a specific distance over a specific time

*resistance:* opposition to displacement

*torque:* force that produces rotation

*velocity:* speed; displacement divided by the time over which it occurs

*weight:* force produced by gravitational attraction

# Index / References to illustrations are in boldface.